UTH
OR
LL
ME

The Resurrection:
Its message and meaning

Ian S McNaughton

DayOne

Printed in 2021

ISBN 978-1-84625-683-7

Unless otherwise indicated, Scripture quotations are from the New
King James Version (NKJV)®. Copyright © 1982 by Thomas Nelson,
Inc. Used by permission. All rights reserved.

British Library Cataloguing in Publication Data available

Published by Day One Publications
Ryelands Road, Leominster, HR6 8NZ
Telephone 01568 613 740 FAX 01568 611 473
email—sales@dayone.co.uk
web site—www.dayone.co.uk

Cover design by Kathryn Chedgzoy
Printed by 4Edge

To all who love the Lord's-Day-Sabbath
and worship in Spirit and truth.
Also to Joel my first grandson born in 2020.

ENDORSEMENTS

This book meets a need for clear teaching about an important, but often neglected, part of the redemption story. The writer expertly draws together verses from both testaments to show that the resurrection was predicted in the Old Testament and was historically documented in the New. Equally valuable and edifying are the chapters on the intermediate state and the ongoing mediatorial ministry of the ascended Christ as our Great High Priest. It exposes the many erroneous beliefs about the state of the soul after death, highlighting the errors of the cults as well as the Roman Catholic belief in purgatory. There is much here to warm the soul as well as to enlighten the mind and I recommend it most heartily.'

Rev. Robert Beckett, Ph.D., Dip.Th., minister of the Evangelical Presbyterian Church in North Belfast

The resurrection is the most important topic—the one that differentiates our faith. Ian McNaughton's book is really important. Victory over death is the most profound victory of any kind. In the same way that science cannot create life (it is too complex) so science cannot resurrect life. Ian's breakdown of sections is just right. Also good is how Ian deals with Islam and its view. It is important to clarify that only Christianity has the true message. One thing that often strikes me is that the modern secular world does not even discuss the possibility that Jesus rose from the dead. The only respectful way of being a 'Christian' today (in the eyes of the world) is to not believe in miracles! So to focus on that key event is a good thing for today.

Professor Stuart Burgess, B.Sc. (Eng.), Ph.D., C.Eng. F.I.Mech.E

In this book by Ian McNaughton we are helpfully reminded of the significance of the resurrection and the change of the Sabbath Day to the First Day of the week. This is the inevitable consequence of the resurrection of the Lord Jesus Christ, God the Son. The challenge and consequences of the resurrection are emphasised and its significance, not only for the true believer, but for all mankind. There are very few recent books that cover this great event in such an assured and confident way. It will be a great resource for busy pastors and theological students to sharpen their understanding of this great event and its significance. But it will also be of blessing to all believers to strengthen their faith and raise their eyes to the glory that awaits those who long for and look for His appearing.

Rev. Dr Ian M Densham, pastor Emeritus of Droylsden Independent Church, Manchester

I wish to recommend this book which throws welcome light on the way Christ's resurrection has, in God's plan, adjusted the Sabbath from the last to the first day of the week. It also has clear teaching on important related subjects, including the evidence for the truth of Christ's resurrection; Christ's intercession now in glory; the future resurrection day for all mankind. These are all subjects of vital relevance to our modern generation. Ian McNaughton's book is an excellent piece of work. He is faithful to Scripture and faithful to the doctrine of the resurrection of our Blessed Lord. It is very much what unbelieving modern readers need to study. I wish it every blessing and hope this first-rate book will soon be available to us all to buy. It shows how precious are these truths about Christ. It will help the reader to see why many thousands of people, past and present, have believed in Jesus Christ as the Saviour of the world. We live in an age of unbelief. People hope that what the Bible tells us about Jesus Christ is not true. The consequence of unbelief is that the teachings of the Bible are treated as religious fiction. I therefore urge you to read this book, which sets before the reader vital truths about Christ's life, death and resurrection.

Rev. Maurice Roberts, Free Church of Scotland; Continuing

The resurrection is the greatest event that ever took place. Through the Resurrection the Lord Jesus Christ is declared to be the Son of God with power. There can never be too many books about the Resurrection, but it is surprising that there are so few. This book by Ian McNaughton addresses that need. It is timely, devotional and thoroughly scriptural, no one can fail to be enriched and instructed through this book. Ian McNaughton brings a lifetime of preaching and pastoral experience together in this book. He provides some unique insights into that most vital of all subjects: the Resurrection of the Lord Jesus Christ from the dead. You will learn from this book: I commend it to you.'

Professor Steve Taylor, Liverpool University and part of the eldership team of Dovecot Evangelical Church

6 The Resurrection

CHART NO. 1   12

CHART NO. 2   18

CHART NO. 3   29

CHART NO. 4   48

CHART NO. 5   51

CHART NO. 6   60

CHART NO. 7   69

8 The Resurrection

Contents

PREFACE   11

INTRODUCTION   15

1 THE GREATEST STORY EVER TOLD   21

2 RIDE ON TO DIE   31

3 THE RESURRECTION: THE THIRD DAY   40

4 THE RESURRECTION: ITS REALITY   52

5 THE RESURRECTION FORETOLD   61

6 THE RESURRECTION: WHAT DID OTHERS SAY?   70

7 THE INTERMEDIATE STATE   82

8 THE RESURRECTION: ITS BLESSINGS   94

9 THE RESURRECTION AND THE LORD'S-DAY   105

10 THE ASCENDED SAVIOUR   116

11 HEAVENLY INTERCESSION   128

12 RESURRECTION CHALLENGE
(1 COR. 15:21–34)   139

13 RESURRECTION CHANGE
(1 COR. 15:35–58)   149

14 RESURRECTION DAY   162

APPENDIX 1: RESURRECTION, THE CULTS
AND SOUL-SLEEP   178

APPENDIX 2: RESURRECTION AND ISLAM   190

APPENDIX 3: MATTHEW 27:45, 52–53   195

BIBLIOGRAPHY   206

10 The Resurrection

It has been said by one of our greatest twentieth century contemporary theologians that, 'Christ redeemed the whole person, and thus the consummation of redemption must involve the redemption of the body (Rom. 8:23; cf. Eph. 1:14)'.[1] The truth of the resurrection of Jesus of Nazareth is fundamental to the message of the Christian gospel that has been sounded out since the Day of Pentecost in the first century AD. It has been the inspiration to all who believe it to be true and the hope of all who by faith have put their trust in God's Son, our Saviour Jesus Christ. The Apostle Paul—writing to encourage the church in Corinth in the spring of AD 55 or 54, and at the beginning of his third missionary journey—knew how important the resurrection of Jesus is to the Christian message of eternal life. Wanting to cheer the church there, he said, 'my beloved brethren, be steadfast, immovable, always abounding in the work of the Lord, knowing that your labour is not in vain' (1 Cor. 15:58).

This book has been a labour of love and comes from the desire to remind contemporary Christianity that if Jesus Christ be not raised then 'there is no resurrection of the dead, then Christ is not risen. And if Christ is not risen, then our preaching *is* empty and your faith *is* also empty' (1 Cor. 15:13–14). However, there is more: the resurrection story is '*His-story*' and the one day in seven Lord's-Day is a witness and continuing sign that he is alive and in session at the right hand of the Father on high. This is accepted, but its importance is neglected in backslidden Christendom. Roman Catholicism does not need a one-day-in-seven Lord's-Day for gathered worship as it celebrates the mass seven days a week. However, Protestantism, of whatever form, is dependent on first day gatherings for worshipping, edification, witnessing and for its survival as a nationally recognised entity which declares the miracle and glory of Jesus Christ's death and his victory over death by resurrection offered to all in the Gospel's presentation.

Having started with the above cause in mind I found that it was necessary to set the Lord's-Day—Sabbath in its historical context and its theological framework. Scholars still debate the exact year that Christ was born which was 6–4 BC and certainly he was crucified between AD 26 and 36 when Pontius Pilate was governor of Judea. Jesus is thought to have been *c.* 33 years old when he died, however not everyone agrees. These disagreements do not weaken the reality that Jesus Christ was a historical figure, which has both biblical and non-biblical contemporary warrant. To help with the 'His-story' I have produced some charts—timelines and harmonies—which set out the dates and events that are relevant to Jesus's birth, death and resurrection.

General

When speaking about the church I use capital 'C' for the universal Church and use its lower case ('c') for the local churches. My concise definition

CHART 1
IMPORTANT DATES

In AD 525 pope John 1 commissioned a new calendar for the Western Church to move away from one based on the founding of Rome (754 BC—YOR).[2] Dionysius Exiguus (who was to prepare the new calendar) characterised the year Jesus Christ was born as AD 1—there is no year zero in this scheme, so the year AD 1 immediately follows the year 1 BC. The date of Jesus's birth is therefore based on Dionysius' calendar date and as secular history tells us that King Herod the Great died in YOR 750 and the New Testament tells us that Jesus was born before his death so Jesus was born 6–4 BC. The chart below sets out an overview of suggested dates.

~ The chart below gives named authors' dates ~

Author	Birth date	Date of crucifixion AD	Age at death years	Day of death (April)	Resurrection AD
Frank Morison	?	30	?	Friday (14 Nisan)[3]	Sunday (16 Nisan)
William Hendrickson	5 BC[4]	30[5]	34/35[6]	Friday (15 Nisan)[7]	Sunday 17 Nisan
Colin J Humphreys	5 BC	33[8]	36/37[9]	Friday[10] (14/15 Nisan)[11]	Sunday 16/17 Nisan[12]
Others	6/4 BC	30	33–36	Friday Nisan 15	Sunday 17 Nisan

of 'Church' is that; it is universal in its extent; local in its expression and personal in its experience (I concede that this is how an independent Baptist might define it!). The idioms 'church militant' and 'church triumphant' are used as might be expected in Protestantism. The use of the phrase 'the Lord's-Day—Sabbath' is of my making but it is not setting out any idea other than that taught in our Protestant confessions of faith. The use of the word 'Sabbath' in the New Testament always indicates the seventh day of Jewish rest. I title the Christian day of rest the 'Lord's-Day –Sabbath' because it is the day of spiritual worship *and* physical respite and it holds dominical authority as such (Rev. 1:10; cf. Mark 2:27–28). I use the idioms, 'saint/saints' as practiced in Protestantism i.e. for those who are God's children saved by faith alone (e.g. Rom. 1:7; Phil. 1:1). I have of necessity discussed the Roman Catholic doctrine of purgatory as it has great bearing on the topic of the Intermediate State of souls between heaven and earth. This Roman tenet has no place in Reformation theology, as the Bible gives no warrant for prayers for the dead.

Thanks

I wish to give thanks to those who have looked over this manuscript and to those who have willingly commended it to God's Church. I am especially grateful to Professor Steve Taylor and Dr Ian Densham and my publisher for advice given. Last but not least, I am indebted to Violet my wife who has prayerfully and patiently supported me in this task (Prov. 31:10).

Rev Ian S McNaughton

2020

NOTES

1 John Murray, *Collected Writings*, Vol. 2 (Edinburgh: The Banner of Truth Trust, 1977), p. 412.
2 YOR, 'The Year of Rome'.
3 Frank Morrison, *Who Moved the Stone?* (OM Publishing, 2001), p. 15.

4 William, Hendriksen, *Survey of the Bible* (Darlington: Evangelical Press, 1995), p. 65.

5 Ibid. p. 66.

6 cf. Luke 3:23.

7 William, Hendriksen, *The Gospel of John* (London: The Banner of Truth Trust, 1969), p. 227.

8 Colin J Humphreys, *The Mystery of the Last Supper* (Cambridge: Cambridge University Press, 2011), pp.71–72. Humphreys however acknowledges that 50% of "modern biblical scholars" support AD 30. The division is related to the secular understanding of the actual date of Tiberius' appointment, AD 12 or 14, (p. 203, n. 19).

9 Humphreys, *The Mystery of the Last Supper*, pp. 72–3, cf. Luke 3:1.

10 Ibid. p. 61, but Humphreys prefers, Nisan 14, p. 69.

11 Ibid. p. 68. This was the day the Passover lambs were slain, p. 68 (cf. 1 Cor. 5:17). Thus Jesus death was on the eve of the Passover (c. Nisan 14).

12 This counts as three days in contemporary Jewish parlance, see Humphreys, pp. 22–25, 61.

Mary Magdalene and the other women arrived at the tomb early on Sunday morning to continue the burial preparations on Jesus's body. They expected to find his corpse where they had laid it on the Friday but they found the stone rolled away and the tomb empty; this was so unexpected. The Bible states that an angel of God removed the stone (Matt. 28:2). A short time later, the risen Saviour appeared first to Mary Magdalene. This was the first of at least twelve resurrection appearances recorded for us in the New Testament that took place over a forty-day period before the Christ ascended into heaven to the Father (Acts 1:9).[1]

This was not what the friends had quite expected! Such an event was unheard of even in Jerusalem, the city of God. What could have happened? Their questions were those that we all would ask in that situation, but the answers that they would get would be also unexpected and were (at first) the last thing their minds thought possible! The truth would seem at first to be 'unbelievable' to all who were involved; to coin a phrase, 'When you have eliminated the impossible, whatever remains, however improbable, must be the truth.'[2] The answer to the riddle of the empty tomb is bodily resurrection from the dead.

Mary's companions were as nonplussed as she about the missing corpse and when they thought Jesus's body had been stolen they ran back in the early light of the morning to tell the disciples of their experiences. Mary Magdalene however, remained there full of sorrow and shock: it was her destiny to be the first person to see the risen Christ. Following that encounter, Mary rushed back to the apostles to report that Jesus was alive and that he had risen from the dead. At this Peter and John ran to the garden, went into the tomb and when John looked in he saw grave cloths but no body and believed Mary's account (John 20:8).

Various objections have been voiced against the resurrection, which never formed part of historic Christianity until recently. Some of these are answered in the book below and they can be summarised as follows:

- Mary and the other women went to the wrong tomb.
- The apostles stole Jesus's body.
- The Jews or the Romans stole Jesus's body.
- Jesus only swooned on the cross and revived later to walk out of the tomb and go to India.
- The faith of the disciples was built on visions or hallucination or lies but not on actual physical evidence.
- Someone who appeared to be Jesus (because he looked like him) died in his place.
- It is just a myth and the New Testament is unreliable as history and truth.

We answer these unsupported hypotheses remembering the significance of Jesus's burial and resurrection in that:

- It was the fulfilment of Old Testament prophecy, 'For you will not leave my soul in Hell (Sheol), nor will you allow your holy one to see corruption' (Ps. 16:10).
- The Roman soldiers who certified Jesus as dead when they took him down from the cross were used to this procedure and were sure that he was deceased.
- Jesus's followers took careful note of the location of the new tomb where he was buried. This they revisited on the Sunday morning finding it was empty, thus they became eyewitnesses to Christ's resurrection.
- The reactions of the disciples later on Easter Sunday challenges the insinuation that this was a deliberate hoax: viz. Mary Magdalene's first report to the apostles and the testimony of the two companions on the Emmaus road on the same day and the risen Jesus's meeting with the apostles (except Thomas) with others present.
- The change of Sabbath day from the last to the first day of the week and the emerging church and its survival and expansion

proves that their faith in the event is more than an acceptance of dubious origin.

• The New Testament Gospels and epistles give cardinal importance to the historic accuracy and the absolute necessity of the reality of the third-day resurrection of Jesus Christ from the dead on the first day of the week.[3]

The empty tomb was either a divine work or a human one. It was the bodily presence of Jesus that confirmed the reality of his reappearances. Thus the empty tomb and the eyewitness testimonies prove beyond contradiction and dispute that 'He is risen indeed' (Luke 24:34). Added to this, the transformation in the attitudes of the witnesses and their boldness in the face of danger shows a moral courage that is unexpected if all was a delusion and a lie. As E F Kevan says, 'the documentary sources of the evidence of the resurrection of Christ may be classified as follows: (1) the history of the Acts, (2) the record of the Gospels, and (3) the writings of Paul. Documents such as these are more than sufficient for the most rigorous demands of scientific investigation.'[4] 'The witnesses are unimpeachable, and the evidence is indestructible, and the conclusion is inescapable.'[5]

There was of course more to the apostles' faith than hearsay. Thus four things were essential to their faith: (i) they had firsthand knowledge of the glory of Christ (John 1:14); (ii) they were witnesses to the resurrection (John 20:1ff); (iii) they had the inner witness of the Holy Spirit (John 14:26; 15:26); and (iv) they possessed the Old Testament Scriptures. Herman Ridderbos puts it well: 'the Gospel is not the story of the later faith of the Christian church; it is the report of the revelation of God in the flesh. But only the end, the resurrection and the Sprit teach disciples to understand the beginning and to offer faith a foothold "in the word that Jesus had spoken"'.[6]

All told the origin and growth of the Christian religion is irresistible proof that God's Word is true and God's Son came into the world to redeem the lost over 2,000 years ago. We are convinced that God's salvation is by faith alone through Jesus Christ alone to the glory of God alone; who cannot lie. The New Testament resurrection narratives are consistent with Old Testament prophecies and the on-growing revelation from Jehovah to Israel under the Old Covenant dispensation. All Scripture oracles are fulfilled in Jesus of Nazareth the incarnate Son of God, the Servant King and promised Messiah with signs that recognised him as the Son of Man in prophecy. Old Testament resurrection hope is consistent with the New Testament's teaching on life after death, giving us ample proof for its affirmation. The people of God regarded death as a heavenly blessing that awaits the resurrection day (John 11:24).

CHART 2 HARMONY OF JESUS CHRIST'S RESURRECTION APPEARANCES DURING THE FORTY DAYS UNTIL HIS ASCENSION			
No. and order	Person/People	NT Text	Place
1	To Mary Magdalene1[7]	Mark 16:9–11 Luke 24:10 John 20:11–18	Jerusalem on the first day of the week (the Lord's-Day)
2	To the group of women who visited the sepulchre	Matt. 28:9–10 Luke 24:1–11 Mark 16:1–8	Jerusalem on the first day of the week
3	To the eleven, and apostle Simon Peter (Cephas) and John	(Matt. 28:8) Luke 24:12, 34, John 20:1–8 1 Cor. 15:5a	Jerusalem on the first day of the week
4	The two disciples on the Emmaus road (one was Cleopas)	Luke 24:13–31 Mark 16:12–13	Jerusalem on the first day of the week

5	The apostles except Thomas with others	Mark 16:14 Luke 24:36–49 John 20:19–25	Jerusalem on the first day of the week
6	The apostles and Thomas (a week later)	John 20:26–31	Jerusalem on the (second) Lord's-Day (Sunday)
7	The seven by Sea of Tiberius (Galilee)	John 21:1–23	Galilee
8	The Great Commission to the eleven disciples	Matt. 28:16–20 Mark 16:15–16 1 Cor. 15:5b	Mountain in Galilee
9	To above 500 at the same time	1 Cor. 15:6	Galilee
10	To James (the Just) Jesus brother martyred AD 62[8]	1 Cor. 15:7a	unknown
11	To the eleven with others on ascension day	Mark 16:19f Luke 24:50–53 Acts 1:2–9 1 Cor. 15:7b	Mt. Olivet
12	To Paul 'as one born out of due time'	Acts 9:3–6; 22:6–10; 26:12–18 1 Cor. 15:8	Damascus road

NOTES

1 See my chart No. 2.

2 Sir Arthur Conan Doyle, stated by his fictional character Sherlock Holmes.

3 Dr Luke, author of the third Gospel and the book of Acts and Pilate the Roman governor at that time are historical, not fictitious, persons.

4 E F Kevan, *The Resurrection of Christ: Dr G Campbell Morgan Memorial Lecture, Number 13*, 1961), p. 4.

5 Ibid. p. 16.

6 Herman Ridderbos, *The Gospel of John* (Grand Rapids, MI: W B Eerdmans Publishing, 1997), p. 121.

7 Mary Magdalene is generally regarded as the first witness to the risen Christ. It is has been suggested that an unnamed servant of the priest was at the tomb before Mary Magdalene and the other women and he was mistaken for an angel (Mark 16:5–7) but on comparison with (Mark 14:27–28, 51–52) this conclusion is not correct. See Frank Morison, *Who Moved the Stone?*, pp. 175–179, 192, for this hypothesis.

8 For a helpful discussion see, Morison, *Who Moved the Stone?*, pp. 125–131.

The greatest story ever told

The resurrection is the most important article of our faith. (John Calvin)

The notion that the believer has been raised with Christ brings into view all that characterises him as a result of him having been joined to Christ as *resurrected*. It means that he has been justified, adopted, sanctified, and glorified with Christ, better, that he has been united with Christ who is justified, adopted, and sanctified, and glorified, and so by virtue of his (existential) union shares these benefits. (Richard Gaffin)[1]

Stories make the world go round (or so we are told). They communicate knowledge and build trust. They speak of life and death and love and hope. They are powerful and at times exciting; 'Anthropologists *tell* us that storytelling is central *to human* existence … *We* use *stories to* make sense of *our* world and *to* share that *understanding* with *others.*'[2] However, when it comes to something as challenging and astonishing as the resurrection of Jesus Christ from the dead on the third day it is often said, 'I want to have proof that this is true' and so, like doubting Thomas, many want to see before they will believe. This book is written as a call to faith and worship because it is about the greatest story ever told, viz. the resurrection of Jesus Christ from the dead.

Biblical history is the door which opens personal salvation and its key is *His-story*. God has given a written record of the life and death of His Son who came into the world—born of a virgin. Providing *His-story* is the most important bequest that parents can give to their children, and God has made sure all who are alive know the truth about Jesus Christ which is essential when death beckons to remove weary pilgrims away. The Bible is God speaking to us in a way that is clear and understandable.

Chapter 1

William Tyndale (the man who translated most of the Bible into English) said a ploughboy would be able to understand it in the vernacular and he gave his life in that pursuit.[3] The gospel story of Jesus Christ's first advent was witnessed to by reliable observers, and his birth, ministry, miracles and passions, as well as his resurrection, are recorded for us accurately in the New Testament. The ancient scribes have preserved *His-story* for us in thousands of ancient manuscripts (this is a miracle in itself if we will receive it). Since the invention of the printing press, publishers have produced millions of copies of Scripture for us to read in many languages so all will believe that, 'God so loved the world that He gave his only begotten Son, that whoever believes in Him should not perish but have everlasting life' (John 3:16). This surely (*His-story*) is the greatest story ever told!

The four Gospels

Mary Magdalene reported to Peter and John that Jesus was alive after meeting the risen Saviour in the garden tomb for herself. On hearing Mary's story they both ran to the garden tomb and looked inside for evidence that her story was not fictitious. When John—who was there first—looked, he saw Jesus's grave clothes lying empty of the corpse and believed. From John chapter 20 we learn that John was the first apostle among the male disciples to believe in Jesus's resurrection. We read, 'He saw and believed' (John 20:8). John saw the empty grave clothes of Jesus where the body was laid but they were devoid of a cold corpse—they lay flat and empty. The handkerchief that had been around his head, which covered his face was seen 'not lying with the linen cloths, but folded together in a place by itself' neat and tidy and certainly *not* where one would expect it to be if the corpse revived and left. If Jesus was rejuvenated in the cool of the night and got up, the linen that was around his body would have been lying in a heap and not as John saw it: this is picture proof of the resurrection. Alternatively, if the body had been stolen the grave clothes would be missing along with the missing body (where one goes, the other would go too). However, they were neat and tidy, undisturbed with the facial handkerchief folded together in a place by itself. The clothes were there but the body was gone! John believed Mary's story but he also believed the evidence of the empty tomb:

John, stooping down and looking in, saw the linen cloths lying *there*; yet he did not go in. Then Simon Peter came, following him, and went into the tomb; and he saw the linen cloths lying *there*, and the handkerchief that had been around His head, not lying with the linen cloths, but folded together in a place by itself. Then the other disciple, who came to the tomb first, went in also; and he saw and believed. (20:5–8)

The body of their Teacher was missing but the grave clothes being undisturbed in location confirmed that the removal was not with human hands. Later, John also believed that the Saviour had risen having a new (spiritual) body suggestive of his previous earthly body but full of spiritual power. This identified Jesus as *the* person who was crucified, buried and died on the cross, namely Jesus of Nazareth. He was risen indeed!

The historical Jesus

Who was Jesus Christ? The Bible holds the answer to this question. All four New Testament Gospels reveal the historical Jesus. They were written in order that the world would know who Jesus Christ really was and is and what he came to earth to achieve. Ancient historians, such as the Jewish Titus Flavius Josephus (AD 37–*c*. 100) and the Roman Publius (or Gaius) Cornelius Tacitus (AD 56–120), both acknowledged in their writings the historical existence of Jesus of Nazareth. The Bible does more; it records Jesus's works of power, his vicarious atonement and his

God-man nature in a historical context in a distinct epoch of history.[4] Jesus, when born, was laid in a manger in Bethlehem in Judea, yet, no other birth of man or woman or of demigod or of general or king or queen or any other human in the history of the world has had an impact like the incarnate Son of God who became man by the virgin birth. Historic dates and figures surround the Incarnation account of God becoming man. Thus Christ's first advent was history in the making: consider King Herod I of Judea (d. *c*. 4 BC, Matt. 2:3; Acts 12:19–23); Archelaus who reigned as Herod's successor (Matt. 2:22); Caesar Augustus[5] (27 BC–AD 14, Luke 2:1); Quirinius Governor of Syria (*c*. 6 BC, Luke 2:2) and Jesus Christ himself (4 BC–AD 30). Pontius Pilate the Prefect of Judea (AD 26/27–36/37) who is known for adjudicating at the trial and crucifixion of Jesus confirms the authenticity of the Man from Galilee. Pilate is one of twenty-three New Testament figures whose existence has been confirmed by archaeology and they are added to over fifty Old Testament characters that have been identified as historical persons from outside of the Bible. One thing is for sure, these numbers only continue to grow. With the passage of time the Bible is not receding into myth, but is increasingly confirmed as history. Outside [extra-biblical] of literary references (the Gospels, Josephus, Tacitus and Philo) and a few coins bearing his name, there was no archaeological evidence for Pilate until 1961. Archaeologists excavating at Caesarea, on the Mediterranean coast, found a large monumental stone 68 cm high bearing the inscription 'Pontius Pilate, Prefect of Judea'. Pilate had an official residence here, but the stone had been broken down and used as filler in a later building. It was quite 'accidental' that such a record was preserved for modern times.[6]

God's timeline

Jesus came into history when the Messiah would be paid attention to and his followers would spread his words and teachings (even) to the Gentile nations. God sent his Son, 'when the fullness of the time had come' on a mission of mercy and on a mission of love; in the vestments of manhood:

'God sent forth His Son, born of a woman, born under the law, to redeem those who were under the law, that we might receive the adoption as sons' (Gal. 4:4b–5).

This 'fullness of the time' speaks of God's providential moment in world's history for the Messianic plan of redemption to be enacted as foretold:

The Lord Himself will give you a sign: Behold, the virgin shall conceive and bear a Son, and shall call His name Immanuel. (Isa. 7:14; 9:6–7)

For unto us a Child is born, unto us a Son is given; And the government will be upon His shoulder. And His name will be called Wonderful, Counselor, Mighty God, Everlasting Father, Prince of Peace. Of the increase of *His* government and peace *there will be* no end, upon the throne of David and over His kingdom, to order it and establish it with judgment and justice from that time forward, even forever. The zeal of the Lord of hosts will perform this. (Isa. 9:6–7)

This was done so that 'in the dispensation of the fullness of the times God might gather together in one all things in Christ, both which are in heaven and which are on earth, in Him' (Eph. 1:9–10, 21; cf. Col. 1:20). Paul refers here to, 'the dispensation of the fullness of the times' making God's plan clear. As Martyn Lloyd-Jones put it, 'The whole span of time has been divided by the coming of the Lord Jesus Christ into the world. That is the division that is emphasised in the New Testament. The times in which we live are called the last times, "the last days."'[7] This theme of the dividing of time is repeated again throughout the New Testament corpus:

Chapter 1

'Now all these things happened to them [Israel] as examples, and they were written for our admonition, upon whom the ends of the ages have come' (1 Cor. 10:11).

God, who at various times and in various ways spoke in time past to the fathers by the prophets, has in these last days spoken to us by *his* Son. (Heb. 1:1–2)

Time is divided once and forever by his first coming. His mediatorial work in heavenly session will go on until the Second Coming. This is God's original plan of redemption and it will come to completion in the 'last day' (2 Tim. 4:8; 2 Peter 3:12–13; Rev. 6:16–17). The first advent was heralded with the virgin birth, which was a message that the child of Mary, wife of Joseph, was the Son of God incarnate:

So all this was done that it might be fulfilled which was spoken by the Lord through the prophet, saying: '*Behold, the virgin shall be with child, and bear a Son, and they shall call His name Immanuel,*' which is translated, 'God with us'. (Matt. 1:22–23)

Then the angel said to them, 'Do not be afraid, for behold, I bring you good tidings of great joy which will be to all people. For there is born to you this day in the city of David a Saviour, who is Christ the Lord. And this *will be* the sign to you: You will find a Babe wrapped in swaddling clothes, lying in a manger.' (Luke 1:10–12)

Scepticism

Can the story as recorded in the four Gospels be believed? There have been attempts to discredit it. The *Times* on Wednesday 9 July 2008 published an article entitled, 'Ancient tablet casts doubt on the resurrection.' It came from Jerusalem and was written by Sheera Frankel. Its opening paragraph stated, 'The death and resurrection of Christ has been called into question by a radical new interpretation of a tablet found on the eastern bank of the Dead Sea.' This three-foot high tablet, known as 'Gabriel's vision of Revelation' was reckoned to be from the first century BC and was instrumental in questioning the resurrection of Christ. It did so referring 'to a Messiah who rises from the grave three days after his death' and it is claimed that the Christ's apostles knew about this (old) story and it was 'adopted by Jesus and his followers'.[8] Now this is another example of scepticism, questioning the veracity and accuracy of the Gospel records. However, there are some serious problems acknowledged about this hypothesis:

- The stone was written on in ink and not engraved as one would expect on a first-century BC tablet. This has caused some to think that it was over-written.
- Previous scholars who worked with the tablet said that, 'the most controversial lines were indecipherable'.
- It is only an interpretation of the words *supposedly* spoken by the angel Gabriel to a historic Jewish rebel named Simon who was killed by the Romans: 'In three days you shall live, I, Gabriel command you.'
- First century BC or the first century AD? There is room for error here regarding the dating. Especially as the article says we are only speaking about four years before the birth of Christ!
- Interestingly other Jewish scholars have disagreed with this interpretation!

His-story as history

What should Christians say to the negative attacks against the historicity of the resurrection? All four New Testament Gospels reveal the history and passion of Jesus written under the inspiration of God (2 Tim. 3:16). They were written in order that the world would know who Jesus Christ really was, and is, and what he came to earth to achieve (John 20:31). So Christians proclaim *His-story* believing that the fallen sinner is someone who is incapable of unprejudiced, unbiased and impartial thoughts while being hearers of the facts and miracles God set before us in the Scriptures. In John 17 Jesus Christ makes a memorable statement about the Bible saying, 'Your word is truth' (v. 17). Jesus clears up any misunderstanding as to what truth is by saying that God's Word is truth. Christians accept his definition. This [truth] is to be understood as being the sixty-six books of the Old and New Testaments but not the apocryphal books; they form no part of the canon of Scripture and have no authority in the churches. The biblical canon is (now) complete and no addition can be made nor needs to be made to it (2 Tim. 3:16; Gal. 1:8–9). As has been said, 'There are no fresh truths of revelation to be discovered either in nature or in church history and tradition which are not to be found in Scripture.'[9] Tradition and human presumptions have no authority to overthrow God's Word; nor does tradition hold equal status as this would result in the subordination of Scripture to the dogmas of fallible men. We must not be reluctant to accept the written history as well as the theology of the Holy Scriptures. J I Packer put it this way, 'What the Bible says, God says, without error.'[10]

The Bible asks those who believe to 'always be ready to give a defence (apologia) to everyone who asks you for a reason for the hope that is in you, with meekness and fear' (1 Pet. 3:15b). His-story is for us to believe and defend, and Peter certainly implies that the Christian faith is capable of reasonable defence. This means that His-story is true and God is pleased with it and the children of God, therefore, are to embrace it by faith and repeat it with joy. Bible prophecy teaches that in the future Jesus Christ will come again a second time, and then every eye will see him, no one will doubt and all will know the truth of the gospel. At the Judgement Day the door of salvation will be closed. Today is the day of salvation! Today you must choose. The story of the death and resurrection of Jesus Christ has been written down that we might believe and become right with God.

CHART 3 THE LIFE OF JESUS CHRIST: TIME-LINE OVERVIEW		
Date	**Event**	**Reference**
c. March 4 BC	The Incarnation and virgin birth	Isa. 7:14; 9:6–7 Matt. 1:15, 23; 2:1–2; Luke 1:26–38; 2:7–14, 25–33; 3:23–38 John 11–14
March/April AD 8	Attendance (at age twelve years) at the Passover in Jerusalem	Luke 2:41–52
AD 26	His baptism in the river Jordan by John the Baptist	Matt. 3:1–17 Mark 1:13 Luke 3:2–22 2 Peter 1:17
AD 26	The temptations of Jesus	Matt. 4:1–11 Luke 4:1–13
April–December AD 27	His early Judean ministry	John 2:13–4:42
December AD 27–April AD 29	His Galilean and retirement ministry	Matt. 4:12–18:35 Mark 1:14–9:50 Luke 4:14—9:50 John 4:43–10:39
December AD 29–April AD 30	His Perean ministry	Matt. 19:20:34 Mark 8:27–10:52 Luke 9:51–19:27 John 10:40–12:11
31 March AD 30	His entry to Jerusalem	Matt. 21:1–11 Mark 11:1–19 Luke 19:28–48 John 12:12–21
5–6 April AD 30	The crucifixion (Friday)	Matt. 27 Mark 15:1–47 Luke 23 John 19

7 April AD 30	The resurrection (Sunday)	Matt. 28:1–20 Mark 16:1–13 Luke 24:1–49 John 20–21 1 Cor. 15
17 May AD 30	The ascension to heaven	Mark 16:19–20 Luke 24:50–53 Acts 1:9–11
AD 30–present	His session in heaven	Rom. 8:34 Heb. 7:25

NOTES

1 Richard Gaffin, *The Centrality of the Resurrection: A Study in Paul's Soteriology* (Baker Book House, 1978), p. 129.
2 https://www.wired.com/2011/03/why-do-we-tell-stories/
3 He was martyred in 6 October 1536 for his work.
4 Josephus, *The Antiquities of the Jews*, and Cornelius Tacitus, *Annals*, Book 15, both mention Christ as a man convicted by Pontius Pilate during Tiberius's reign.
5 Gaius Octavius—(Octavian).
6 e-n.org.uk/2019/01/regular-columns/pilates-ring/a67a6—Chris Sinkinson, D L Moody Lecturer in Apologetics, Moorlands College.
7 M Lloyd-Jones, *God's Ultimate Purpose* (Banner of Truth, 1978), pp. 199–207.
8 *Times*, Wednesday 9 July 2008, p. 35.
9 D B Knox, *The 39 Articles* (London: Hodder & Stoughton, 1967), p. 22.
10 Scripture is the ultimate and final authority or standard beyond which there is no appeal or criteria. See J I Packer, *God has Spoken: Revelation and the Bible* (London: Hodder & Stoughton, 1985), p. 28.

Ride on to die—death, burial

To be without faith is to be without any ground of hope for the future. It is only by faith that we can have any reasonable ground for expecting any happier state of things in the new world than we have in the present. (William Booth, 1829–1912)

The Old Testament foretold that God would redeem his people through his Suffering Servant (Ps. 22:1, 7–8; Isa. 53) and the New Testament proclaims that Jesus Christ, who was crucified on the cross, buried and resurrected on the third day, is that Promised One (Acts 24:15, 21).

The final week

The Gospel writers devoted much of their material to the events leading up to the resurrection of Jesus. The final week of his earthly ministry began with the triumphal entry into Jerusalem and the shouts of 'Hosannas' from the assembled crowd. This later changed into cries of 'crucify Him' before the week was over when Jesus presented himself openly to the Jewish people as their Messiah and their true King. This was in fulfilment of the prophecy of Zechariah 9:9:

Rejoice greatly, O daughter of Zion! Shout, O daughter of Jerusalem! Behold, your King is coming to you; He *is* just and having salvation, Lowly and riding on a donkey, A colt, the foal of a donkey.

Jesus had travelled south from Galilee knowing that the time of his death (as the 'Lamb of God') was near and he enters into the den of wolves, which is Jerusalem, to be harassed and betrayed and killed. The time is the spring of AD 30. He might have spent the Sabbath (Saturday) in Bethany ('the house of dates') with Lazarus whom he had raised from the dead and his sisters Mary and Martha (John 12; Luke 19). It is now on the first day of the week and he has a two mile walk to Bethphage ('house of figs') and then on by foot to the Mount of Olives, 2,600 feet a.s.l. (c. 790 metres). From there he looks down over Jerusalem where he must die as our substitute and Redeemer. Having reached this place he sends two of his disciples to retrieve a donkey with its colt, which He told them they would find tethered. They were to 'borrow' it and bring the unbroken animal to him. If anyone challenged them, they were to say, 'The Lord has need of them' (Mark 11:3). The disciples found the colt tied outside in the village and they did as Jesus commanded them (Matt. 21:6). Though the colt had never been ridden before, it did not recoil at carrying Jesus into Jerusalem. As he entered, a carpet of clothes and tree branches was made (Mark 11:8), and as he rode the people cried, 'Hosanna! Blessed is He who comes in the name of the Lord' (Mark 11:9), which originally meant *Save, we pray*, but which later became an exclamation of praise. That they cried, 'Blessed is He who comes in the name of the Lord' (Ps. 118:26a); a clear recognition that Jesus was fulfilling the messianic promise that day.[1]

Ride on ride on in majesty

If Jesus was to fulfil his incarnate destiny, he must declare himself as the promised Messiah and be seen by all Israel fulfilling the prophetic words from Ps. 118:26a:

Blessed is he who comes in the name of the Lord!

His death was not to be hidden but a public event: His death was for all to see, as John said (19:36–37 and quoting the prophecies of Ps. 34:20; Zech. 12:10):

For these things were done that the Scripture should be fulfilled, 'Not one of His bones shall be broken.' And again another Scripture says, 'They shall look on Him whom they pierced.'

His entry into the city on the colt was seen, remembered and recorded. He then went into the Temple and looked around 'at all things' and as it was late in the day he travelled back to Bethany with the twelve and returned again the next day (Mark 11:11). John later wrote:

He who has seen has testified, and his testimony is true; and he knows that he is telling the truth, so that you may believe. (John 19:35)

What lessons lie here for us?

(1) GOD'S PLAN OF REDEMPTION WAS REVEALED

On the day when Jesus rode into Jerusalem on the colt of a donkey, He was fulfilling God's divine plan of redemption. This was a clear sign that Jesus was the promised Messiah and that the promised One had indeed come into the world as foretold in the Scriptures. This historical moment along with his mode of transport—that of princes and kings—a donkey (Judg. 5:10; 10:4; 12:14; 2 Sam. 16:1–2)—sealed the heavenly sign (Zech. 9:9). However, Jesus's kingdom was not of this world. His journey was to Golgotha, not to a palace or a parliament but to a cross and to a cruel death (the 'Way of Suffering'—cf. Isa. 50:4–6). After his resurrection on the third day Jesus ministered another forty days before his ascension.

The Bible gives to us the historical record of the out working for the Covenant of Redemption to save the world from the first announcement—*protoevangelium*[2] (Gen. 3:15)—to the coming of Messiah by the Incarnation; death on the cross and resurrection from the dead on the third day and all that followed on from this. It was planned and it was carried out as ordained from eternity and it was achieved so that the second Adam, Jesus Christ once raised for the dead, would, 'become the firstfruits of those who have fallen asleep. For since by man came death, by Man also came the resurrection of the dead. For as in Adam all die, even so in Christ all shall be made alive' (1 Cor. 15:20–22). We are meant to remember and believe in Christ's messianic mission to save us. In John 17:20, Jesus, knowing the importance of this to posterity, prayed, 'I do not pray for these alone [the disciples], but also for those who will believe in Me through their word.'

(2) THE BIBLE'S PROPHECIES WERE FULFILLED AND THE EYEWITNESSES BELIEVED
When Jesus rode into Jerusalem on the colt he went into the city and was met by a large crowd (Matt. 21:8,9 –'a very great multitude') and they cried out, 'Blessed is the kingdom of our father David that comes in the name of the Lord! Hosanna in the highest!' (v. 10). The eyewitnesses to Christ's passion and resurrection were divinely chosen and were with Christ from the beginning (John 1:14; 1 Peter 3:2–4). They were promised the assistance of the Holy Spirit in order to truthfully and accurately record *His-story* for future generations (John 14:26; 15:26; 2 Peter 1:20–21). Following Jesus's resurrection the disciples (eyewitnesses) were afraid because they were accused of stealing the body. However, after Pentecost they preached on the foundation of the historical reality of the resurrection without fear. This all Christians must do also. The truth of the resurrection is made known in the Scriptures and is to be told of (gossiped) by all who believe. The Bible is a reliable historical document and we have the original texts copied and preserved from the autographs.[3] It is fixed and final and it cannot be added to or changed. So we must work with the text we have been given and from it we must learn about Jesus's humanity and try to understand his Trinitarian union. God wants the world to know and believe in his Son and to believe in his saving work (John 3:16). History records no Jesus Christ and Saviour other than the one who is presented to us in the New Testament (Acts 4:12).

The people in Jerusalem on Palm Sunday thought that the kingdom of

God was about to be set up with Jesus Christ sitting on a throne of David, so they cried, 'Blessed is the kingdom of our father David that comes in the name of the Lord.' However, it was not quite as they had been taught by the Pharisees. The promised Messiah was predicted to be a son (descendant) of King David and they rightly made the connection (the Gospel of Matthew provides the legal lineage from David through Joseph to Jesus (1:1–17), while the Gospel of Luke (3:28–38) provides the physical lineage from David through Mary to Jesus). He has appeared in Jerusalem with a public demonstration of his prophetic mandate and He is made welcome. This story was the fulfilment of (OT) prophecy and the apostolic eyewitnesses are its messengers and guarantors.

(3) PRAISE WAS GIVEN TO JESUS

We are all called to praise the Lord who came to save us. On that day when Jesus rode into Jerusalem on the colt of a donkey the crowd cried, 'Hosanna! Blessed is he who comes in the name of the Lord!' (Mark 11:9). What excitement and what joy were known there. What anticipation and hope it engendered. Also, what gospel truth it communicated. He was now to be recognised for who he really was. Secrecy was no longer necessary for that would work against his witness and destiny as the Messiah and Saviour.

Jesus comes into public view in order to die a public death. The very next day he will go into the temple and drive out those who bought and sold and exchanged money and cheated the poor (Mark 11:15). It will not be long until he is brought, yes, forced to walk publicly carrying his cross to the place of death and there to be crucified before eyewitnesses and doubters. He has a destiny to fulfil and a world to save. Matthew tells us that, 'a very great multitude' was in Jerusalem at the Passover (21:8). These pilgrims and residents were also to be the eyewitnesses who would tell their contemporaries about the Lord's coming to save. Matthew tells us 'all the city was moved' (21:10). There was that day, a public stirring and an: (i) appeal of prayer: 'Save, we pray'; (ii) anticipation of promise: 'save now'; (iii) an acclamation of proclamation: that Jesus is Messiah and King; and (iv) an adoration of praise: because He was coming in the name of the Lord (Jehovah). This public cry of 'Hosanna', speaks of Jesus Christ's own name as Saviour and in the name of the Godhead—the Three in One, Father, Son and Holy Spirit. This was Jesus's triumphant procession for he rode to die seeking victory over death and hell (which was guaranteed) because Jesus Christ is God's Son, Saviour.

Ride on ride on in majesty,
In lowly pomp ride on to die.

Good Friday

Crucifixion was one of the most terrible forms of torture ever devised. It was most probably used by the Persians, the first known being in 519 BC when King Darius crucified 3,000 political opponents in Babylon. It was then adopted by Alexander the Great and his successors including the Seleucid Empire (which covered the Levant), and later by the Romans.[4] The word comes from the Latin *crucifigere* which means 'to fix to a cross'. Crucifixion was an everyday event in the Roman Empire, but it was not common in Palestine when Pontius Pilate was the Prefect. It was a barbaric mode of capital punishment as it allowed no mercy but rather was designed to inflict maximum pain and suffering. The Romans used it as a punishment for slaves; their own citizens were exempt. The Emperor Constantine I abolished it in AD 315.

While hanging on the cross our Saviour was certified dead quicker than the Romans expected and so his heart was punctured with a spear to make sure the victim did not only appear dead but he *was* dead! The Gospel record tells us this sudden action resulted in the out flowing of "blood and water" from Jesus side (John 19:34) because the heart cannot get the blood from the legs of a crucified victim to oxygenate it and the heart of Jesus would have eventually produced a watery fluid (i.e. blood with no red or white cells in the pericardium membrane that enclosed the heart) and when the Roman spear pierced the Saviour's side the membrane was ruptured and blood and water flowed out. This method of Christ's death was of man's devising, but it was also in fulfilment of Old Testament prophecy. This is seen from Psalm 22, where we read 'all My bones are out of joint ... they pierced My hands and My feet' (vv. 14, 16). This Psalm reads like a contemporary eyewitness narrative yet it was part of the Jewish Old Testament canon written around a thousand years before the time of Christ (compare Matt. 27:39, 43–46). After our Saviour was certified dead his corpse was taken down from the cross by the cruel hands that nailed him there.

Reconciliation

In the plan and purpose of God, Jesus died vicariously atoning for sin and achieving reconciliation between God and fallen humankind:

Jesus our Lord ... was delivered up because of our offenses, and was raised because of our justification. (Rom. 4:24–25)

Calvin points out that 'Sin is the cause of enmity between God and us; and, until it is removed, we shall not be restored to the Divine favour. [However], it has been blotted out by the death of Christ, in which he offered himself to the Father as an expiatory victim'.[5] The death of Christ reconciled sinners to God. This Paul writes about in Colossians chapter one speaking of man's depravity, so when he talks of being reconciled to God he is preaching the gospel:

You, who once were alienated and enemies in your mind by wicked works, yet now He has reconciled in the body of His flesh through death, to present you holy, and blameless, and above reproach in His sight. (Col. 1:21–22)

Reconciliation means a resolution of problems and a restoration of friendship between those who are out of fellowship. Propitiating reconciliation is rooted in Christ's death. It was the Father who sent the Son to Calvary. On the cross the Son was judged, sentenced and punished on our account to establish peace between us, believing sinners, and God. The ultimate aim of reconciliation is the removal of God's wrath and the presentation of believers as 'holy, and blameless, and above reproach in His sight' (see also Rom. 3:25; 1 John 2:1–2). Robert Murray M'Cheyne spoke of Christ's atonement thus, 'God heaped upon his Son all our sins until there was nothing but sin to be seen. He appeared all sin; nothing of his own beauty appeared … he [was] willing to be made sin for us, and this was His love'.[6]

His burial

The Gospels give us the facts regarding Christ's burial. His body was placed in a new tomb owned by a rich man called Joseph of Arimathea.[7] Here Christ lay until the third day. A guard was placed at the tomb at the request of the Jewish hierarchy and with the agreement of Pontius Pilate so that the body would not be stolen. The significance of his burial is threefold. Firstly, it was the fulfilment of Old Testament prophecy; (i) in Psalm 16:10, King David said, 'For You will not leave my soul in Sheol, nor will You allow Your Holy One to see corruption', yet David himself was buried but did not rise from the dead. These words were quoted by the Apostle Peter on the Day of Pentecost (Acts 2:31) as proof that Jesus Christ was the promised and awaited Messiah of the Jews; (ii) it proves that the Romans soldiers had certified Jesus as dead when they took him down from the cross. They were used to this procedure and were sure that he was deceased; and (iii) Jesus's followers took careful note of the location of the tomb where he was buried and on the Sunday morning when they arrived it was empty; thus they became eyewitnesses to Christ's resurrection.

NOTES

1 The Greek word for Lord (*kurios*) is the word use in the LXX (Greek OT, translated for the exiled Jews between 3 BC and AD 5) for the Tetragrammaton: Jehovah/YAWH. Thus it has all the force of the eternal divine name.

2 'In Christian theology, the *protoevangelium* is God's statement to the serpent in the Garden of Eden about how the seed of the woman would crush the serpent's head: "And I will put enmity between thee and the woman, and between thy seed and her seed; it shall bruise thy head, and thou shalt bruise his heel"' (https://en.wikipedia.org/wiki/Protevangelium). This is not to be confused with *The Gospel of James*, also known as the *Protoevangelium of James*, which is an apocryphal gospel probably written around the year AD 145.

3 Extant manuscripts exceed 5,000 copies. See Appendix 5 of my book *Engaging with Islam: an evangelical perspective* (Day One, 2019).

4 Patrick Sookhdeo, *Hated without a Reason* (McLean, VA: Isaac Publishing, 2019), p. 15.

5 John Calvin on Eph. 2:16, *Commentary in John Calvin Collection* (CD_Rom; Christian Library series; Rio, WI: AGES Library, 2007).

6 Robert M M'Cheyne, *God Made a Path*, ed. Stanley Barnes (Belfast: Ambassador Productions Ltd., 1997), p. 103.

7 Jewish burial custom prescribed that the body of the departed be washed and oiled, the hair cut and tidied, the corpse dressed again and the face covered with a cloth.

The Resurrection: The third day

Jesus said to them, 'The Son of Man is about to be betrayed into the hands of men, and they will kill Him, and the third day He will be raised up.' (Matt. 17:22–23)

As you look at the resurrection you are looking at a victor. (Dr Martyn Lloyd-Jones) [1]

Holy Week begins with Palm Sunday and Jesus's final week of earthly ministry began with the triumphal entry into Jerusalem and the shouts of 'Hosannas' from the assembled crowd. However, this later changed into cries of 'crucify Him' before the week was over. As we noted above the (predestined) time had arrived for Jesus to present himself openly to the Jewish people as Messiah their true King. He did this in fulfilment of the prophecy of Zechariah 9:9:

Rejoice greatly, O daughter of Zion! Shout, O daughter of Jerusalem! Behold, your King is coming to you; He *is* just and having salvation, Lowly and riding on a donkey, A colt, the foal of a donkey.

Monday and Tuesday

Having spent Sunday night in Bethany, Jesus and His disciples return to Jerusalem (Mark 11:12–14) on Monday morning and came to the Temple:

Jesus went into the temple and began to drive out those who bought and sold in the temple, and overturned the tables of the money changers and the seats of those who sold doves. (Mark 11:15)

The cleansing of the temple was a startling act by which the Jews discerned the messianic claim of Jesus and accordingly they sought a sign from Jesus. They confronted him with a question, 'what sign do you show to us?' Jesus answered and said to them, 'destroy this temple, and in three days I will raise it up' (John 2:18–19). John makes it clear that the 'sign' would be Jesus's resurrection from the dead (John 2:21–22). Christ Himself would raise the 'temple of his body' on the third day according to the Scriptures. This verse agrees with the Synoptic Gospels where Jesus pointed to His resurrection as the only sign that would be given to the Jews:

An evil and adulterous generation seek after a sign, and no sign will be given to it except the sign of the prophet Jonah. (Matt. 12:39; 16:4; cf. Luke 11:29–30)

Those who do not believe in the resurrection refuse to accept that Jesus was in the tomb for three day and nights and endeavour to interpret the biblical text in a way that contradicts the New Testament's testimony. They try to interpret the phrase, 'the sign of the Prophet Jonah' as contradicting the idea of three days. In their attack the obvious meaning of Christ's words are spun out of all proportion (John 2:18–22).

Wednesday or Thursday?

There has been much controversy over the actual *day* of the week of Christ's Passover meal with his disciples. Most scholars agree Thursday evening but others (a minority) suggest Wednesday. The Gospels agree that Jesus died the day before the (Jewish) Sabbath, hence Jesus died on a Friday and that it is consistent with Jesus rising on the third day (Sunday). The ancient Jews counted the resurrection day from and including the day of burial, thus three days. *Whichever day is judged to be correct does not affect the reality of a third day bodily resurrection.* The day of the

Lord's Supper followed Judas' agreed plot with the Jews to betray Jesus (cf. John 18:28).[2]

Good Friday

The day Jesus was crucified, Joseph of Arimathea, a secret disciple of the Lord Jesus and a member of the Sanhedrin (Mark 15:43; Luke 23:50–56), went to Pilate and asked if he might have the privilege of receiving the body of Jesus when it was taken down from the cross in order to give it a suitable burial (this was between 3 and 6 pm). Permission was granted, and Joseph promptly wrapped it in linen aided by others and laid it in his empty unused tomb that was hewn out of the rock. This happened on (Good) Friday, the day of the Preparation as the Sabbath drew near (we are to remember that the Jewish Sabbath begins on Friday at sunset):

> A rich man from Arimathea, named Joseph, who himself had also become a disciple of Jesus. This man went to Pilate and asked for the body of Jesus. Then Pilate commanded the body to be given to him. When Joseph had taken the body, he wrapped it in a clean linen cloth, and laid it in his new tomb which he had hewn out of the rock; and he rolled a large stone against the door of the tomb, and departed. (Matt. 27:57–60; cf. Lk. 23:50ff)

On the Saturday Sabbath the women rested, in obedience to the commandment concerning *Shabat*.

The third day

When Jesus told the Jews he would be three days and three nights in the earth, they took this to mean that the fulfilment of the prophecy could be expected after only two nights. On the day *after* his crucifixion, that is, after only one night (Friday), they went to Pilate and said, 'Sir, we remember how that impostor said, while he was still alive, "After three days I will rise again" and asked that he "commanded the sepulchre to be made secure until the third day' because the Jewish hierarchy feared that his body might shortly go missing (Matt. 27.63–64). Jesus's resurrection on the third day was prophetically foretold by Jesus himself (Mark 8:31; 10:34; Matt. 16:4, 21; 20:19; Luke 9:22; 18:33). This could not have been accomplished except by God raising him up and it could not have been according to the Scriptures except it fulfilled the Old Testament prophecies (1 Cor. 15:3-4; see above chapter 2).

Contemporary Jewish terminology

The phrase 'the sign of the Prophet Jonah' is found in Matthew 12:39–40 and Luke 11:29 (cf. John 2:19). It is part of the repeated narrative of our Lord during his teaching ministry with the apostles. The fact that it is repeated in the Gospels signifies its importance to the plan of redemption and the gospel message. It lays emphasis on the time Christ was in the tomb before he arose bodily at his resurrection and the resurrection as a sign that tells the world that Jesus Christ is Lord. The stated 'third day' is to be noted as correct as it confirms the bodily resurrection in its prophetic fulfilment. That Jesus was buried for three days is confirmed by the Hebrew inclusive reckoning of time where days are counted whether in whole or in part: 'How can it be said that He was three days and nights in the tomb? The answer is that, in Jewish reckoning, any part of a day and night counts as a complete period. "A day and a night make an *onah*, and a part of an *onah* is as the whole (Jewish saying)".'[3] Friday to Sunday is to be reckoned and counted as three days and three nights by Hebrew common parlance and tradition. The Jews took any part of the day as the whole day when counting up a time period in first-century Palestine. Jesus's first appearance to the apostles and the women on the resurrection day (Sunday) was followed by a second appearance 'after eight days'. This in the Jewish vernacular was one week later (i.e. our seven days). Which means the risen Christ appeared a second time to them a week later:

And after eight days His disciples were again inside, and Thomas with them. Jesus came, the doors being shut, and stood in the midst, and said, 'Peace to you!' Then He said to Thomas, 'Reach your finger here, and look at My hands; and reach your hand *here*, and put *it* into My side. Do not be unbelieving, but believing.' (John 20:26–27)

The sign of Jonah (fulfilled) is Christ's resurrection on the first day of the week.[4] We were told that the dead Jesus would be in the tomb three days because the Jews took any part of the day as counted in when counting up a time period. A fine example of this ancient approach is found in the Book of Esther where Queen Esther said, 'neither eat nor drink for three days, night or day' (Esth. 4:16) but on the third day, when only two nights had passed, she went into the king's chamber and the fast was ended. 'St Augustine finds this particular sign instructive for understanding the nature of signs. Augustine reads the sign of Jonah as a part which signifies a whole, namely the resurrection of Christ. He tells us that this is a particular example of a kind of figure of speech called a *synecdoche*, in which the part can either be read for the whole or the whole for the part (i.e., continuity in the relation of signs).'[5] The third day has been challenged by Islamic scholars' as well as by liberal Christian theologians. However, allowing for Jesus being buried on Friday after having been certified dead by the Roman centurion's cohort (a band of battle-hard executioners trained by Rome to kill its enemies with the utmost cruelty) and that he had hung on the wooden stake for nine hours with thieves each side and he in the middle (John 19:14, 31, 38, 42) secures the time frame when our risen Lord was seen early on the Sunday morning by Mary Magdalene and the other women: i.e. three (Jewish) days later. Jonah's experience of being swallowed by the great fish and then disgorged (Jon. 1:17; 2:10) prefigured the Lord's passion and resurrection. His rising from among the dead would be the final, climactic sign of Jesus's ministry to the nation of Israel and the world.

Resurrection Day appearances

On resurrection Sunday evening the disciples were assembled together. This is—in my estimation—his fifth appearance after He rose from the dead on that resurrection day and it corresponds with the account in Luke 24:36–48 when the doors were shut for fear of the Jews.[6] Unexpectedly they saw Jesus standing in the midst (v. 36). Luke tells us that the two disciples whom the risen Jesus met on the Emmaus Road were with them and they were all, 'terrified and frightened, and supposed they had seen a spirit' (vv. 33–35). The Gospel narrative accounts show us how the risen Christ proved to His followers—something they did not initially want to accept—that He was not an apparition or a hallucination. This proof was necessary in order to empower them mentally and psychologically to preach His resurrection victory and glory to come when facing persecution and martyrdom later:

Jesus Himself stood in the midst of them, and said to them, 'Why are you troubled? And why do doubts arise in your hearts? Behold My hands and My feet, that it is I Myself. Handle Me and see, for a spirit does not have flesh and bones as you see I have.' When He had said this, He showed them His hands and His feet. But while they still did not believe for joy, and marvelled, He said to them, 'Have you any food here?' So they gave Him a piece of a broiled fish and some honeycomb. And He took *it* and ate in their presence. (Luke 24:38–43)

Sixth appearance: after eight days

Doubting Thomas' response to his personal meeting with the resurrected Saviour eight days later fits with the prophetic statements of Jesus given to the disciples about his coming resurrection. In John 20 we observe Jesus meeting the apostles and he persuades them that he is risen indeed. Thomas, having heard from the eyewitnesses that Jesus was alive, made a personal choice to remain sceptical until he was persuaded otherwise. John's narrative account of Thomas's mind-set tells the story:

Now Thomas, called the Twin, one of the twelve, was not with them when Jesus came. The other disciples therefore said to him, 'We have seen the Lord.' So he said to them, 'Unless I see in His hands the print of the nails, and put my finger into the print of the nails, and put my hand into His side, I will not believe.' (20:24–25)

After eight days (*kai meth hemeras hokto*) 'He said to Thomas, "Reach your finger here, and look at My hands; and reach your hand *here*, and put *it* into My side. Do not be unbelieving, but believing"' (v. 27).

Thomas's answer is memorable and extraordinary; looking at the risen Jesus Christ he said, '"My Lord and my God!" Jesus replied, "Thomas, because you have seen Me, you have believed. Blessed *are* those who have not seen and *yet* have believed"' (vv. 28–29). You will note that even after his resurrection Jesus still exhibited and possessed the puncture marks of the cross (v. 20). This is instructive as it showed to Thomas and the others with him the 'Stigmata of Redemption' which Jesus alone must carry. Now, the homicidal effect of sin and its destructive powers are removed by; sin's wounds; sin's bruises; sin's griefs and afflictions (Isa. 53):

He *was* wounded for our transgressions, He *was* bruised for our iniquities; The chastisement for our peace *was* upon Him, And by His stripes we are healed. (Isa. 53:5)

Jesus had waited for a week ('after eight days', v. 26) to reveal the (chosen) new Sabbath. It is pertinent to ask now why is there no record of activity or historical narrative between the resurrection day and the eighth day appearance. Could it be that we now have the seventh day Sabbath passing away and the first day Sabbath instituted by the Lord Jesus Christ himself (Rev. 1:10)?

Five irrefutable proofs
These narratives show five irrefutable confirmations given to the apostles that Jesus Christ 'had risen indeed':

- The assembled cohort heard with their own *ears* Jesus's welcome voice: with their own *ears* they heard him saying, 'Peace be with you' (Luke 24:36; John 20:19).
- The assembled cohort saw with their own *eyes* the awful nail prints in his body and the injury caused by the Roman spear. 'Behold My hands and My feet that it is I Myself' (Luke 24:39a; John 20:27). Here Christ's once physical body is now changed to take on immortality and incorruptibility with a power over nature's rules, but it was the same body in which he died and was buried (Luke 24:38; John 20:20).
- The assembled cohort also *watched* Jesus eat fish and honey, 'But while they still did not believe for joy, and marvelled, He said to them, "Have you any food here?" So they gave Him a piece of a broiled fish and some honeycomb. And He took *it* and ate in their presence' (Luke 24:41–43). They watched him thus proving utterly that he was not an angel or apparition or hallucination.
- The assembled cohort were challenged to *touch* his hands and feet, 'Handle Me and see, for a spirit does not have flesh and bones as you see I have. When He had said this, He showed them His hands and His feet' (Luke 24:39b). Doubting Thomas was also offered the same proof (John 20:27).
- The assembled cohort experienced the inner witness of the Holy Spirit, John tells us that, 'He breathed on *them*, and said to them, "Receive the Holy Spirit"' (John 20:22). Luke said, 'He opened their understanding, that they might comprehend the Scriptures' (24:45–44); this he had also done with the two disciples on the Emmaus road (v. 31).

Thus we see here the risen Saviour providing proof of His resurrection without delay. He does so first on the resurrection day itself by using the natural senses of the apostles and the disciples present—their touch, hearing, seeing and attentiveness. These reluctant believers came to the realisation that what was impossible for men was possible with God the Almighty. He answered their doubts and fears, thus empowering them to preach His passion, atonement and His resurrection for our justification with conviction and great effect (Acts 2; 1 Thess. 1:5).

A new Sabbath: the Lord's-Day

Jesus waited for a week (John 20:26) before he met with the disciples (again) and this time with Thomas present. He chose to do so, on the first weekly anniversary of the resurrection day. We do not think that this was anything other than deliberate with lasting intentions and lessons for the apostles as this day (the first day of our calendar week) is now called by all the Church the Christian Lord's-Day (Rev. 1:10). His timing is very significant and was the start of a new sanctified pattern of worship and change of Sabbath Day, which became the tradition of the first church in Jerusalem. 'After eight days' reveals the chosen new Sabbath established by our Lord himself and is now the time of New Covenant worship. The Saviour had, by his carefully selected presence, sanctified their coming together with his presence. This was the start of Sunday worship and it became the custom of the churches after the ascension.

Turning to Acts 2:1 on the Day of Pentecost, 'When the Day of Pentecost had fully come, they were all with one accord in one place' we find the disciples all together again and this was also on the first day of the week for Pentecost was always on the next day after the seventh-day Sabbath. John Bunyan (the Baptist preacher) is convinced that the phrase 'after eight days' confirms this day is the chosen new Sabbath established by the Holy Spirit.[9] This model of worship which was new to Jewish converts can be seen in Acts 20:7 when the apostle and the saints, whilst at Troas, came together to break bread on the first day of the week (Sunday). Paul had been there for a few days and on the Lord's-Day he established the new pattern of apostolic worship with the breaking of bread (the Lord's Supper) and preaching. This was a remembering of the Lord's death *till He comes* (1 Cor. 11:26).

CHART 4 EMPTY TOMB WITNESSES			
Name	At the cross on Friday	Noted the correct tomb (Friday)	At the opened tomb on Sunday (Lord's-Day)
Mary Magdalene (Luke 8:2)	Matt. 27:56, 61 Mark 15:40, 47 Luke 23:49 John 19:25	Matt. 27:56, 61 Mark 15:47 Luke 23:55-56	Matt. 28:1 Mark 16:1 Luke 24:1, 10 John 20:1, 11–18
Mary wife of Clopas	Cf. Matt. 27:55 Cf. Mark 15:40 Cf. Luke 23:49 John 19:25		Cf. Luke 24:10
Salome, mother of James and John, Zebedee's sons[7]	Matt. 27:56, 61 Mark 15:40 John 19:25	Matt. 27:56 Mark 15:40 cf. Luke 23:55–56	Matt. 28:1 Mark 16:1 Luke 24:1, 10
Mary, the mother of James the Less and Joses	Matt. 27:56 Mark 15:40, 47	Mark 15:40, 47 Luke 23:55–56	Matt. 28:1 Mark 16:1 Luke 24:1, 10
Mary, the mother of Jesus, wife of Joseph[8]	John 19:25	x	x
Joanna, wife of Chuza, Herod's steward (cf. Luke 8:2 and 3)	Matt. 27:55	?	Luke 24:1 and 10
Apostle John	John 19:26–27	(John 20:4)	John 20:2–4 and 8
Apostle Peter	?	(John 20:4)	Luke 24:12 John 20:2–6
Joseph of Arimathea (Mk. 15:43 and Lk. 23:51)	Mark 15:43–46 John 19:38–42	✓	x
Nicodemus (John. 3:1)	John 19:39–42	✓	x

Chapter 3

This continuation of a new day of worship was established by the apostles after Pentecost (Acts 2:44–47) and adopted as the new day of worship in the provinces of Asia. Paul, writing to the Corinthians, makes it clear that the gathering of the people of God *on the first day of the week* was now the preferred time of weekly worship (1 Cor. 16:1, 2).[10]

NOTES

1 Tony Sergeant, *Gems from Martyn Lloyd-Jones* (Milton Keynes: Paternoster, 2007), p. 251.

2 C J Humphreys contends that the Last Supper was on the Wednesday of holy week and this 'allowed just the right amount of time to fit in all the events the gospels recorded as happening between the last supper and the crucifixion' (*The Mystery of the Last Supper*, p. 195). William Hendrickson differs saying, 'it is clear, therefore, that Jesus and his disciples celebrated Passover at the proper and customary time; i.e., on Thursday night' (*Survey of the Bible*, p. 166).

3 *The Believer's Bible Commentary*, Nelson Study Bible CD_ROM.

4 See my book *The Real Lord's Prayer: Christ's Glory and Grace in John 17* (Leominster: Day One, 2012), for a fuller treatment of this issue.

5 www.etext.virginia.edu/journals/ssr/issues/volume3/number1/ssr03-01-e05.html

6 The disciples were afraid because they were accused of stealing the body, however, after Pentecost they preached on the foundation of the historical reality of the resurrection empowered by the Holy Spirit and assurance.

7 A sister of Mary Jesus' mother, cf. William Hendriksen, *The Gospel of John* (London: The Banner of Truth Trust, 1969), pp. 431–432.

8 Mary the mother of Jesus was not a witness to the resurrection. This is very interesting and is relevant to the debate in the Church about her status. Salome was perhaps with John while he supported the mourning Mary after Jesus' death.

9 John Bunyan (1628–1688), 'Questions about the Nature and Perpetuity of the Seventh-Day Sabbath', *The Works of John Bunyan* (London: Blackie and Son, 1861), Vol. 2, p. 374.

10 For early Christians, Sunday, as well as being the first day of the week, was also the spiritual day of worship but the change of day had no effect on the use of the seven-day week for calendar purposes: 'The first day after the Sabbath, remaining the first of all the days, is called, however, the eighth, according to the number of all the days of the cycle, and [yet] remains the first' (Justin Martyr, *Dialogue with Trypho*, chapter XLI). This does not set up an eight-day week, since the eighth day is also considered to be the first day of the next weekly cycle.

CHART 5 HOLY WEEK TIME-LINE	
Day	**Events**
Sunday	• Jesus enters Jerusalem on an ass's colt (Luke 19:29–44)
Monday	• Triumphant entry into Jerusalem (Matt. 21:1–11; Mark 11:15; Luke 19:45–48) • The cleansing of the temple (Matt. 21:12–13; Mark 11:15–17; Luke 19:45–48) • The cursing of the barren fig tree (Matt. 21:18–19; Mark 11:19–26)
Tuesday	• Jesus foretells the destruction of Jerusalem (Matt. 23:37; Luke 19:43–44; 21:24) • Mary anoints Jesus at Bethany (John 12:2)
Wednesday	• Judas [perhaps] consults with the Jewish rulers to betray Jesus for thirty pieces of silver (Matt. 26:14–16; Mark 14:10–11; Luke 22:3)
*Thursday	• Jesus eats the Passover meal with His disciples and institutes the Memorial Supper on the first day of unleavened bread (John 13:1; Mark 14:12; Luke 22:7; John 19:30). • Jesus makes his High Priestly payer (John 17)
Friday	• Jesus prays alone in the Garden of Gethsemane (Matt. 26:36–46; Mark 14:32–42; John 18:1) • Judas betrays Jesus and he is arrested (Matt. 26:47–56; Mark 14:43–50; John 18:2–11) • Peter denies Jesus (Matt. 26:57–58, 69–75; Mark 14:53–54, 66–72; John 18:15–18, 25–27) • Jesus is beaten and tried (Mark 14:65; 15:1–5; Matt. 27:1–2, 11–14; 26:67–68; 27:1; Luke 23:1; 21–24; John 18:28–38) • Jesus is mocked and crucified between two thieves (Matt. 27:31–56; Mark 15:20–41; Luke 23:28–49; John 19:16–30) • The veil of the temple is torn in two as Jesus dies (Matt. 27:51) • Jesus is buried in the tomb of Joseph of Arimathea (Luke 23:50–56; John 19:31)
Saturday	• A guard was posted with the consent of Pontius Pilate (Matt. 27:65)
Sunday (Lord's-Day)	• The guards at the tomb are scattered and bribed (Matt. 28:4, 12–13) • An angel says that he is risen indeed' (Matt. 28:2, 5–7; Luke 24:2–6) • Jesus is raised from the dead and appears to around seventeen witnesses that day (Matt. 28:9; Mark 16:9; Luke 24:1–11; John 20:14–16)

*'Jesus and his disciples celebrated Passover at the proper and customary time; i.e. on the Thursday night' (Hendriksen, *Survey of the Bible* (Darlington: Evangelical Press, 1995), p. 166).

The Resurrection: Its reality

The Christian faith stands or falls with the resurrection of Christ. (Ernest F Kevan)

These things were done that Scripture might be fulfilled. (John 19:36)

T he resurrection of Jesus Christ lies at the very heart of the Christian faith; take it away and all that is left of Christianity is another religion whose founder is dead and buried and whose teachings can be superseded in the years to come. However, all honest readers of the Bible must agree that Scripture teaches without reservation or contradiction that Jesus Christ arose from the dead on the third day and that that day was the first day of the week (Sunday). The Jews, Romans and Christians at the time all agreed that:

- Jesus Christ was dead when taken from the cross;
- He was buried in a new tomb;
- On the third day his body was missing from the tomb; and
- The disciples of Jesus deny removing his body; the Jews and the Romans also deny being the tomb robbers.

Where had the body gone? When the women arrived at the tomb early on Sunday morning to continue their burial preparations on Jesus's body expecting to find his corpse where they had laid it three days before, instead they found the stone rolled away and the tomb empty (Luke 24:1–3). The Bible states that an angel of God had removed the stone (Matt. 28:2). A short time later, the risen Saviour appeared to Mary Magdalene. The Bible proclaims the authenticity of Christ's resurrection, but it does not attempt to describe the process. It simply tells us what happened and expects us to believe it. Those who reject the truth of Christ's resurrection reject the testimony of the Holy Scriptures seeing it as unreliable and they often charge its writers (the apostles and prophets) with deception and dishonesty. One thing is clear however, the Bible never doubts the resurrection of God's Son from the dead. The disciples were afraid of the Roman authorities because they were accused of stealing the body. However, after Pentecost they preached on the facts of the historical reality of the resurrection with boldness. The truth of the resurrection is made known in the Scriptures. We have the manuscript texts which have been given to aid understanding and generate faith.

The empty tomb was either a divine work or a human construct. E F Kevan says, 'the enemies of Jesus had no motive for removing the body: the friends of Jesus had no power to do so. It would have been to the advantage to the authorities that the body should remain where it was; and the view that the disciples stole the body is impossible.'[1] Thus the empty tomb and the eyewitness testimonies prove beyond contradiction and dispute that, 'He is risen indeed' (Luke 24:34). Added to this, the transformation in the attitudes of the witnesses with their boldness in the face of danger testifies to a new moral courage that was astonishing if it all was a delusion and a lie; 'The witnesses are unimpeachable, and the evidence is indestructible, and the conclusion is inescapable.'[2] Their willingness to die bearing testimony was because of the Holy Spirit given at Pentecost (Acts 2; cf. 1:8). Resurrection is the triumph of Jesus Christ over death 'the last enemy' (1 Cor. 15:26). Because of this, believers can be confident that they will rise on the last day. Christ has defeated Satan who had the power of death. This power was taken from him at the cross (Col. 2:14; Heb. 2:14–15). Jesus made this possible by his own resurrection on the third day. It is clear there were Jews like Martha, the sister of Lazarus, who believed in a resurrection to come (John 11:24) and when it comes to the twenty-seven books of the New Testament the careful readers can only come to one conclusion, viz. that Jesus Christ arose from the dead on the third day. Some may not want to believe, nevertheless that is what is written within.

(i) The New Testament believes in the resurrection

When examining chapters 27 and 28 of the Gospel of Matthew it is clear that:

- Christ's disciples came into contact with the dead body of Jesus when it was taken to the empty tomb (Matt. 27:57–61; cf., Luke 23:50–56): A "rich man from Arimathea, named Joseph, who himself had also become a disciple of Jesus … went to Pilate and asked for the body of Jesus. [And] Pilate commanded the body to be given to him. When Joseph had taken the body, he wrapped it in a clean linen cloth, and laid it in his new tomb which he had hewn out of the rock; and he rolled a large stone against the door of the tomb, and departed" (Matt. 27:57–60).
- The Romans and Jews agreed that Jesus Christ really died when on the cross. The Romans took Jesus's corpse down from the cross believing him to be dead and a watch was set over the tomb where he was buried (Matt. 27:62–66).
- The Jews were party to covering up the problem of the missing body. If they or the Romans had removed Jesus corpse they could have disproved the resurrection claim of the Christians later on. The disciples were utterly perplexed at first as to the whereabouts of his body when they found the tomb empty (Matt. 28:5–8; cf. Luke 24:1–12).
- The Romans, Jews or the disciples of Jesus did not remove the body. The guards reported it missing (Matt. 28:4, 11–15). The Jewish authorities bribed the soldiers who reported (to them) with a large sum of money to say that the body was missing and they were asked to lie about the event and blame the disciples of Christ (Matt. 28:11–13).
- The apostles, however, were very reluctant to believe that Jesus was now alive and the words of the first witnesses seemed like idle tales and they did not believe it at first (cf. Luke 24:11).

From the above it is clear that the Bible accepts as true that Jesus Christ rose again three days after he was buried. It never doubts the testimony of the eyewitnesses who heard it first from the angel (Matt. 28:5–7) and then met the risen Saviour for themselves before telling their story to others (Matt. 28:9–10).

(ii) The New Testament deliberately praises the Resurrection

The story of Christ's resurrection is given top place in the recorded miracles of the Bible for it outshines even the supernatural raisings from death of Lazarus, Jairus's daughter and the widow of Nain's son (John 11; Luke 7:11–12; 8:55). They were brought back from the dead but were certain to die again and be buried to await the general resurrection at the last day. However, Christ's triumph over death was the beginning of an endless life glorified in heaven. It was the accomplishment and the consummation of the Incarnation. At the Incarnation he became man— for he took a body and 'he had an immortal and rational soul' and now remains the God-man forever.[3] The resurrection is not in 'the likeness of sinful flesh' (Rom. 8:3) but is a renovate humanity in the power of an endless life. It is manhood, made new, and restored (1 Cor. 15:47–49).

(iii) The New Testament simply witnesses to the resurrection

It is remarkable that the facts of Christ's resurrection are given with an attempt to describe the act in great detail. It is with minimal scope we are told what happened and left to believe it or not! The narrative accounts of this miracle do not record the metaphysical or biological or spiritual processes undertaken to make the resurrection of a body possible. The dead Saviour was missing and the Bible says, 'He is not here; he is risen' (Matt. 28:6). This is evidence of the inspiration of the Bible. If false witnesses had written it, the accounts would probably contain detailed descriptions of what was happening during the exchange from death to new life but not so the inspired book of God. The Bible proves the reality of the resurrection by listing the twelve or so post-resurrection appearances of Christ to his followers until his ascension as recorded in the first chapter of the book of Acts (Chart 2). The post-resurrection appearances can be found by harmonising the four accounts in the Gospels and chapter 15 of First Corinthians. They are the accounts of eyewitnesses to his new form and resurrection realities. The Bible is remarkable and unique in proclaiming both His disappearance and His appearance as it reveals the One who achieved the prophetic goal of resurrection and offers to those who believe a share in His triumph. The Bible reveals that the resurrection body will be a real body but not according to the flesh but according to the Spirit (1 Cor. 15:45).

1 Corinthians 15

In First Corinthians we are told that Christ's resurrection *is* the gospel (vv. 1–2). Here Paul asserts that the denial of the resurrection constitutes a complete overthrow of the faith, so to deny the resurrection is to disavow the gospel of our Lord Jesus Christ. However, under the inspiration of the Spirit he lays out the essential proofs for us:

For I delivered to you first of all that which I also received: that Christ died for our sins according to the Scriptures, and that He was buried, and that He rose again the third day according to the Scriptures. (1 Cor. 15:3–4)

The eyewitnesses to the resurrection are listed by Paul BC 25 years after Easter in the spring of AD 55. Then there were possibly still as many as 521 living eyewitnesses (excluding the women) to the bodily resurrection of Jesus Christ and Paul makes mention of them and includes himself in that list:

He was seen by Cephas, then by the twelve. After that He was seen by over five hundred brethren at once, of whom the greater part remain to the present, but some have fallen asleep. After that He was seen by James, then by all the apostles. Then last of all He was seen by me also, as by one born out of due time. (vv. 5–8)

This list included the doubting Apostle Thomas whom we know took a week (eight days) to accept the fulfilment of Old Testament prophecy. The utter legitimacy of the apostle's reports were only accepted when Jesus appeared to him personally on the second Lord's-Day after the resurrection (John 20:27–28; cf., Rev. 1:10). The witness testimonies of the women can be read in the later chapters of the Gospels.[4] Paul's own (Damascus Road) experience can be read in the Book of Acts (9:3–8; 22:6–11; 26:12–18). However, in First Corinthians Paul says, "then last of all He was seen by me also, as by one born out of due time" (v. 8). The experience Saul had on the Damascus Road so altered him that he was never the same again. Instead of judging, persecuting and executing believers he joins with them and thereafter was always willing to suffer and die for his risen Saviour (Acts 8:3; 9:1–9; 2 Cor. 11:22–29).

These personal testimonies are the foundation of the Christian Church's witness to the greatest story ever told.[5] It appears Nathanael of Cana in Galilee was also a witness to Christ's resurrection. We first find him in John's Gospel chapter one, 'Jesus saw Nathanael coming toward Him, and said of him, "Behold, an Israelite indeed, in whom is no deceit!"' (v. 47). Nathanael was so taken with this encounter that he 'answered (Jesus) and said to Him, "Rabbi, You are the Son of God! You are the King of Israel!"' (v. 49). After three years had passed Nathanael ('of Cana in Galilee') was still a disciple with Peter, Thomas called Didymus and two other disciples and he shared a resurrection encounter in Galilee. This was Jesus third appearance to the disciples *as a group* and (perhaps) the seventh chronologically (John 21:1–14).[6]

The confirmation

Paul in the First epistle to the Corinthians clarifies for us that the Old

Chapter 4

Testament prophesied the resurrection of Jesus and that the New Testament eyewitness accounts confirm the historic reality of the resurrection and so he lays out an authentic weight of evidence on the soundness of the resurrection claim in chapter 15. Old Testament prophecy and history are two great allies which declare the miracle of Christ's resurrection on the third day. But what of the doubt that arises in many hearts? What of unbelief that lingers in sceptical minds? Paul speaks to this:

Now if Christ is preached that He has been raised from the dead, how do some among you say that there is no resurrection of the dead? (v. 12)

To the Greeks and the early Gnostics the idea of bodily resurrection was strange and incompatible with their own philosophical ideas (Acts 17:32). The Greeks believed that man's body was only an evil or a fetter or a dungeon or grave (*soma-sema*; 'body tomb') from which death frees the soul.[7] Paul, who lived in the light of the Scriptures, rejected these ideas and argues for the proof and legitimacy of Old Testament prophesy. He declares to his readers that the implications of rejecting the resurrection of Jesus on the third day are gargantuan. To deny its possibility is gospel-denying and faith-destroying, because:

If there is no resurrection of the dead, then Christ is not risen. And if Christ is not risen, then our preaching *is* empty and your faith *is* also empty. (vv. 13–14)

By 'empty' Paul means 'vain' (*kenon*); it has no purpose. If Christ failed to rise and was defeated and if he is dead and his body corrupted in the grave then we are all doomed to dwell in corruption forever. If this were true:

We [Paul and the apostles] are found [to be] false witnesses of God, because we have testified of God that He raised up Christ, whom He did not raise up—if in fact the dead do not rise. (v. 15)

Such a reality (Paul argues) would result in the silencing of the public proclamation of Christian truth and hope for sinners because all 'are still in their sins.' If the resurrection is a lie, hope has no purpose. Hope originates from faith and faith justifies the sinner before God (it is imputed to them) because Christ, 'was delivered for our offences, and was raised for our justification' (Rom. 4:25) [AV]. To be 'still in your sin' is to be guilty still, condemned still, dead to God still, and facing hell for eternity still, now hope is lost and lives are doomed, 'Then also those who have fallen asleep in Christ have perished' (v. 18). To perish (*apollumenos*) is to be deprived of salvation and abandoned. It does not indicate annihilation as asserted by some cults and others. 'He who perishes is forever separated from God, heaven, and eternal life. His body and soul share the fate of Satan in the eternal torment of hell.'[8]

Paul's logic is stark, 'If in this life only we have hope in Christ, we are of all men the most pitiable' (v. 19). However, Paul and the witnesses to the resurrection looked forward while sharing hope and peace through the gospel. Jesus's resurrection is about tomorrow; the 'what next' and is the 'not yet' that is promised to those who know God. So God's people are to live by faith, walk in faith and pray for the salvation of the lost while letting our brief lives be shaped by gospel grace that offers hope to all fallen humanity. This is the reality; it was prophesised, it is historically witnessed and it is a certainty because, 'Christ is risen from the dead, *and* has become the firstfruits of those who have fallen asleep' (v. 20).

Christians are to evangelise using this good news as time is short and we are told, 'It is appointed for men once to die, but after this the judgment' (Heb. 9:27). People are to be exhorted to believe in the resurrection and to pray for themselves while, 'it is yet day—for the night is coming'.

CHART 6 'MARY' THE NAME OF SIX WOMEN IN THE NEW TESTAMENT
Mary the mother of Jesus, wife of Joseph (Matt. 1:16). There is no scriptural proof that she vowed to be or was of perpetual virginity (Mark 3:31; 6:3; Matt. 1:25; 13:55; Luke 8:19–29; John 2:12; 7:5).
Mary Magdalene, the woman from whom Jesus cast out seven demons and first witness to the resurrection (Lk. 8:2; 23:55–56; John 19:25; 20:1, 11–14).
Mary, sister of the Virgin Mary, the wife of Clopas who was a witness to the crucifixion and burial tomb (Mark 15:40, 47; Matt. 27:56; Luke 24:10; John 19:25; 20:1). She is mother of James (the Less) and Joses and Salome (Matt. 27:56; Mark 15:40, 47; 16:1; John 19:25).
Mary of Bethany, sister of Martha and Lazarus (Luke 10:38–42; John 11:1–2, 19–20ff).
Mary, the mother of John Mark (Acts 12:12) the mother of the author of the Gospel of Mark.
Mary of Rome (Rom. 16:16). All we know is that she was a helper to Paul and church member in Rome.

NOTES

1   Kevan, *The Resurrection of Christ*, p. 14.
2   Ibid. p. 16.
3   C Hodge, *A Commentary on the First Epistle to the Corinthians* (London: The Banner of Truth Trust, 1964), p. 350.
4   See chart 4.
5   This is why the Bible is constantly attacked!
6   See my 'A Harmony of Jesus Christ's Resurrection Appearances', chart 2.
7   R C H Lenski, *1 and 2 Corinthians* (Minneapolis, MI: Augsburg Publishing House, 1963), p. 624.
8   Ibid. p. 657.

The Resurrection foretold

It is justifiable to affirm that the resurrection of Christ is the primary conviction of the Christian faith. (E F Kevan)

Resurrection hope was not confined to the pages of the New Testament in addition it is found in the Tanakh, Prophets and the other writing of the Hebrew Bible. It is sometimes said that very little is taught in the Old Testament on this topic however, that is a dismissal of the importance of what is given. The New Testament against, all logic and previous human experience, proclaims that Jesus who was crucified rose from the dead on the third day; the tomb being empty.

We have seen above that the Apostle Paul was sure that the Old Testament speaks prophetically about resurrection and that he was convinced that (Jesus) 'rose again the third day according to the Scriptures' (1 Cor. 15:3). The 'Scriptures' for Paul, as a Jew, are very important and as a convert to Jesus the Christ extremely significant for the authenticity and spread of Christianity. They are (for Protestants) to be defined as the Old Testament with its thirty-nine books and nothing more; not the Apocrypha or the Quran or Book of Mormon, etc.[1] The Scriptures go back a long time: Abraham was called by Jehovah God c. 4,100 years ago and Moses the Servant of God c. 3,450 BC.[2] The Scriptures, both Old Testament and New, are the Oracles of God; the writings inspired by the Holy Spirit without which we would not know or understand God and His world and His plan for us in Jesus Christ His Son:

All Scripture *is* given by inspiration of God, and *is* profitable for doctrine, for reproof, for correction, for instruction in righteousness. (2 Tim. 3:16)

Prophecy never came by the will of man, but holy men of God spoke *as they were* moved by the Holy Spirit. (2 Pet. 1:21)

Chapter 5

The Testimony of the Old Testament

The Pentateuch is not as silent as it may at first seem when we remember that Jesus quoted Exodus 3:6 in Matthew 22 to prove that there is life after death for the people of God:

> Concerning the resurrection of the dead, have you not read what was spoken to you by God, saying, 'I am the God of Abraham, the God of Isaac, and the God of Jacob' God is not the God of the dead, but of the living. (vv. 31–33)

The Old Testament therefore predicted the resurrection to come and in the New Testament the eyewitnesses report it as an actual fact (e.g. Job 19:25–27; 1 Sam. 2:6; Ps. 16:9–11; 17:15; Mark 16:1–14; 1 Cor. 15:1–11; Acts 10:39–41). Saul the Pharisee believed in the resurrection before he was saved. Although what he did not believe—until the day of his conversion on the Damascus road—was that Jesus Christ had risen from the dead three days after his burial in the garden tomb.[3]

GENESIS CHAPTER 22

In Genesis (the first book of the Scriptures) we find that Abraham believed in bodily resurrection; this is of first importance, and a harbinger of truth to come:

> By faith Abraham, when he was tested, offered up Isaac, and he who had received the promises offered up his only begotten *son*, of whom it was said, '*In Isaac your seed shall be called*,' accounting that God *was* able to raise *him* up, even from the dead, from which he also received him in a figurative sense. (Heb. 11:17–19)

Abraham was promised a son—the promised seed—through whom the world would be blessed (Gen. 21:12, cf. Gal. 3:16). Calvin said, 'Isaac is not to be thought of as simply one of the common company of men, but as one who contained Christ in himself.'[4] Thus when the command to sacrifice Isaac came,

Abraham had faith to believe that God could raise Isaac from the dead (vv. 8, 15–18; Heb. 11:17–19). The restraining of Isaac is history, but also figurative in the form of a parable or analogy, for he was as good as dead but God provided a ram to sacrifice in his place typifying Jesus our sacrifice (vv.7–9; 1 Cor. 5:7).[5] Abraham's faith possessed the assurance that with God nothing was impossible (Gen. 18:14), even this great miracle (22:5). Here the typical significance of resurrection is seen in the offering of Isaac which begins an ongoing hope promised to God's people through faith. Athanasius (c. AD 296–373), Augustine (AD 354–430), Aquinas, Luther and Theodore Beza all agree.[6] John Owen pointed out, 'Abraham firmly believed not only in the immortality of the souls of men, but also the resurrection from the dead. Had he not done so, he could not have found relief in this distress' (cf. John 8:56).[7]

1 SAMUEL 2

In Hannah's prayer of thanksgiving, she speaks of the sovereignty of God in providence and creation and states her belief in resurrection, 'My heart rejoices in the Lord; My horn is exalted in the Lord' (v. 1). In verse 6 she again refers to God's power to resurrect the dead, 'The Lord kills and makes alive; He brings down to the grave and brings up.' Because God is the Almighty, Hannah understands that He is the arbiter of life and death; he only can give life, and he only has a right to take it away and He makes alive at his will and bidding. Jehovah God brings down to the 'grave'—the Hebrew word *sheol* seems to have the same meaning in the Old Testament with *hades* in the New, which is the word generally used by the Septuagint for the other. Hannah gives us insight into the Hebrew religious mind. She was spiritually minded and renewed in truth or why else could she pray as she does in chapter 2? Christians who are familiar with the New Testament cannot help, when they come across this verse, but think on Lazarus (John 5:28) and the others raised from death by Jesus. However, most of all, it is Jesus's death and resurrection that comes to mind when this verse is read with its reference to death and resurrection. The *Targum* seems to understand (v. 6) of death and the resurrection: 'He kills and commands to give life; he causes to descend into Sheol, that in the time to come he may bring them into the lives of eternity', i.e. the life of shame and everlasting contempt, and the life of glory.[8] Matthew Henry says on verse 6, 'This prophecy looks to the kingdom of Christ, that kingdom of grace, of which Hannah speaks, after having spoken largely of the kingdom of providence. And here is the first time that we meet with the name MESSIAH, or his Anointed. The subjects of Christ's kingdom will be safe, and the enemies of it will be ruined; for the Anointed, the Lord Christ, is able to save, and to destroy.'[9]

THE BOOK OF JOB

The ancient patriarch Job's belief in the resurrection of the body shines through despite all his troubles, pains and difficulties:

For I know that my Redeemer lives, and He shall stand at last on the earth; and after my skin is destroyed, this I know, that in my flesh I shall see God, whom I shall see for myself, and my eyes shall behold, and not another. How my heart yearns within me! (Job 19:25–27)

Job's language is that of the believer. He is convinced that God is his Saviour and that he will see God one day. When he does God will be with his Advocate. On these verses Matthew Henry says, 'Job was taught of God to believe in a living Redeemer, and to look for the resurrection of the dead and the life of the world to come.'[10] During Job's time of illness, bereavements and public rejection, he lost all hope of getting physically better and he did not think that he would live much longer (Job 19:8–10; see also 30:23). However, Job, under the influence of the Holy Spirit, is lifted out of his misery and given an eye to future hope. At this point Job rests in unforeseen blessing while exercising faith and patience. This expectation is founded on the very character of the living God himself (Job 1:21). In chapter 19 and verses 25–27, Job shows that there was grace and light in the hearts of Old Testament saints who embraced resurrection hope. Job lived *c*. 2,100 BC this suggests that belief in the resurrection of the body and eternal life preceded the birth of Abraham. We will see that the Old Testament speaks in many places about the resurrection from the dead. Francis I Andersen's comments are pertinent: 'the argument that Job does not expect personal reconstitution as a man, because this idea entered Judaism only towards the very end of the biblical period, can be dismissed in the light of much recent research that shows interest in the afterlife as an ancient concern for Israelite faith. In particular, the outcome of our study of such passages as Job 14:13ff, if valid, shows that the hope of resurrection lies at the very heart of Job's faith' (cf. Heb. 11:19).[11]

The OT major prophets

Of special interest are Isaiah, Ezekiel and Daniel.

ISAIAH (*C*. 739–686 BC)

The prophet Isaiah spoke of resurrection of the body, 'Your dead shall live; together with my dead body they shall arise. Awake and sing, you who dwell in dust' (Isa. 26:19). This is a reference to personal bodily resurrection and it shows faith in the doctrine and perhaps also a desire for it to happen (now).[12]

EZEKIEL (*C*. 636–586 BC)

In the prophecy of Ezekiel, resurrection was a valid doctrine as appears when God is actively asking questions:

And He said to me, 'Son of man, can these bones live?' So I answered, 'O Lord God, You know.' Again He said to me, 'Prophesy to these bones, and say to them, O dry bones, hear the word of the Lord!' Thus says the Lord God to these bones: 'Surely I will cause breath to enter into you, and you shall live.' (Ezek. 37:3–6)

We see why Pharisees like Saul/Paul accepted that the Scriptures teach resurrection and now we see the reason for Paul's statement, 'Men *and* brethren, I am a Pharisee, the son of a Pharisee; concerning the hope and resurrection of the dead I am being judged' (Acts 24:14–15).

DANIEL (C. 636–530 BC)

In the book of Daniel, prophecy is written between (*c*. 536–530 BC). It is the first time that expression 'everlasting life' appears in the Bible:

Many of those who sleep in the dust of the earth shall awake, some to everlasting life, some to shame *and* everlasting contempt. (Dan. 12:2)

Some commentators see Daniel 12:2 as referring not to physical resurrection but to the national and moral revival of Israel. However, Jesus's own interpretation in the Gospel of John rules this out, when he quotes Daniel and refers to the (general) resurrection:

Do not marvel at this; for the hour is coming in which all who are in the graves will hear His voice and come forth—those who have done good, to the resurrection of life, and those who have done evil, to the resurrection of condemnation. (John 5:28–29)

Daniel's prophecy speaks of resurrection to come and to the Last Judgment at the end of time. It includes believers and unbelievers (cf. Matt. 13:43; 1 Cor. 15:40ff; Rev. 2:28). C F Keil sums it up saying, 'The salvation of the people, which the end shall bring in, consists in the consummation of the people of God by the resurrection of the dead and the judgment dividing the pious from the godless.'[13]

In the OT minor prophets

The resurrection hope is continued in the smaller prophetic books. Of special interest are Hosea, Jonah and Zechariah.

IN HOSEA (*C.* 753–725 BC)

I will ransom them from the power of the grave; I will redeem them from death. O Death, I will be your plagues! O Grave, I will be your destruction! (13:14)

This mighty text is quoted by Paul in his concluding remarks in his monologue on the resurrection (1 Cor. 15:54–55). Jehovah's promised redemption to His chosen people is fulfilled through Jesus Christ's resurrection from the dead: the grave having no power over those in Jesus Christ by faith. By Christ's resurrection, death is defeated and its sting made useless: 'As judgment against Ephraim was irrevocable, so redemption and deliverance from Sheol was unchangeably determined.'[14]

IN JONAH (*C.* 760 BC)

Now the Lord had prepared a great fish to swallow Jonah. And Jonah was in the belly of the fish three days and three nights. (1:17, cf. Matt. 12:40)

This famous text is quoted by our Lord and is found in Matthew (12:39–40) and Luke (11:29–32; compare John 2:18–19). It is part of the repeated narrative of our Lord's teaching ministry with His apostles. The fact that it is repeated in the Gospels signifies its importance in the plan of redemption and to gospel preaching. It lays emphasis on the period that Christ would be in the tomb before He rose on resurrection day and was a sign that tells the world that Jesus Christ is Lord and Saviour.

IN ZECHARIAH (*C.* 520–470 BC)

And I will pour on the house of David and on the inhabitants of Jerusalem the Spirit of grace and supplication; then they will look on Me whom they pierced. (12:10)

Here again the Scripture implies a resurrection to come. Jehovah promises renewal and eternal hope to His people offered in the Covenant of Grace. This authentic reading, 'they will look on Me whom they pierced', points not to Jehovah but to His Son the great Shepherd of the sheep (John 10:14). God's salvation flows from a special (free) grace towards repentant persons bringing, 'an internal light of faith the author of which is the Spirit'. This view of God as Saviour is to be taken metaphorically but applied to the Messiah and fulfilled in Christ.[15] The Apostle John said of when Jesus's side was pierced by a spear on the cross, 'For these things were done that the Scripture should be fulfilled, [and] Scripture says, "They shall look on Him whom they pierced"' (John 19:37), thereby assuring us that resurrection hope was promised in the Old Testament Scriptures.

NOTES

1 See the *Westminster Confession of Faith*, Chapter 1:2. Also the *Congregational Savoy Confession of Faith and the Baptist Confession of Faith 1689*.

2 Hendrickson, *Survey*, pp. 61, 92.

3 The story of Paul's conversion on the road to Damascus is told in Acts 9:1–19 and retold by Paul in Acts 22:6–21; 26:12–18.

4 Philip E Hughes, *Commentary on Hebrews* (Grand Rapids, MI; W B Eerdmans Publishing, 1977), p. 483.

5 We must not think that God intended Abraham to kill his son Isaac for it is evident; (i) if Abraham had refused to obey God then Isaac would not have died; (ii) if on the other hand, as was the case, Abraham was willing to obey and sacrifice Isaac, God, as we read in Genesis, had a plan all along to provide a substitute lamb. This is a great gospel illustration.

6 Hughes, *Hebrews*, pp. 485–486.

7 A W Pink, *An Exposition of Hebrews* (Grand Rapids, MI: Baker Book House, 1979), p. 751.

8 Clark's *Commentary on the Bible*; https://bibleapps.com/commentaries/1_samuel/2-6.htm

9 Matthew Henry, *Concise Commentary*; https://bibleapps.com/commentaries/1_samuel/2-6.html

10 Mathew Henry, *Commentary on the Whole Bible*, Vol. 3, p. 108.

11 Francis I Andersen, *Job: An Introduction and Commentary* (Tyndale Old Testament Commentaries; Nottingham: Inter-Varsity Press, 1976), p. 210.

12 The record of Isaiah's prophecies contains the revelations that God graciously gave during the reigns of Uzziah (792–740 BC), Jotham (752–736 BC), Ahaz (736–720 BC) and Hezekiah (729–699 BC).

13 C F Keil, 'Daniel', in E J Young, *Daniel* (London: The Banner of Truth, 1972), p. 257.

14 Homer Hailey, *The Minor Prophets* (Baker Book House, Grand Rapids, MI, 1978), p. 181.

15 John Calvin, *Commentary: Zechariah and Malachi* (Edinburgh: Banner of Truth Trust, 1986), p. 362. See also ibid. p. 364, note 1.

CHART 7
THE RESURRECTION IN THE OLD TESTAMENT
Genesis 22:18 In your seed all the nations of the earth shall be blessed, because you have obeyed my voice.
1 Samuel 2:6 The Lord kills and makes alive; He brings down to the grave and brings up.
Job 19:25–26 For I know that my Redeemer lives, And He shall stand at last on the earth; and after my skin is destroyed, this I know, that in my flesh I shall see God.
Ps 16:9-11 (Acts 2:27, 31) For You will not leave my soul in Sheol, nor will You allow Your Holy One to see corruption. You will show me the path of life; In Your presence is fullness of joy; At Your right hand are pleasures forevermore.
Ps. 132:11 The Lord has sworn in truth to David; He will not turn from it: 'I will set upon your throne the fruit of your body.'
Isa. 26:19 Your dead shall live; Together with my dead body they shall arise. Awake and sing, you who dwell in dust;
Ezek. 37:3–6 And He said to me, 'Son of man, can these bones live?' So I answered, 'O Lord God, You know.' Again He said to me, 'Prophesy to these bones, and say to them, "O dry bones, hear the word of the Lord! Thus says the Lord God to these bones: Surely I will cause breath to enter into you, and you shall live."'
Dan. 12:2 (John 5:28, 29) And many of those who sleep in the dust of the earth shall awake, some to everlasting life, some to shame and everlasting contempt.
Hos. 13:14 (1 Cor. 15:55) I will ransom them from the power of the grave; I will redeem them from death. O Death, I will be your plagues! O Grave, I will be your destruction!
Jonah 1:17 Now the Lord had prepared a great fish to swallow Jonah. And Jonah was in the belly of the fish three days and three nights (cf. Matt. 12:40)
Zech. 12:10 And I will pour on the house of David and on the inhabitants of Jerusalem the Spirit of grace and supplication; then they will look on Me whom they pierced.

Chapter 6

The Resurrection: What did others say?

He has been raised from the dead, how do some among you say that there is no resurrection of the dead? (1 Cor. 15:12)

There were heresies in the world then, as there are still, which taught that sin only applies to the body, that sin is something physical, and that salvation, therefore, means escaping out of the body. That is the teaching of Hinduism and of Buddhism. The great thing is to escape out of the body, to get rid of the flesh, and the moment you get out of the body, it is said, you leave sin behind. That is the exact opposite of Christian salvation which teaches not the escape out of the body, but the redemption of the body. (Dr Martyn Lloyd-Jones)[1]

T he resurrection of Jesus Christ from the dead lies at the heart of the Christian faith and that is why it receives such special attention in all the four Gospels (Matt. 28; Mark 16; Luke 24; John 20), the Acts (1:1ff), and Paul's epistles, especially 1 Corinthians 15. The resurrection of Jesus Christ is the seal and headstone of the great work of redemption and it is the crowning proof that Christ paid the debt of sin on behalf of the elect and that he won the battle that delivers believers from hell fire.

1. Opposition

We meet the Sadducees in the New Testament. They were mainly members of the priestly order who appear to have accepted only the written law, as distinct from Hebrew tradition. However, they taught that there was no resurrection of the body (Matt. 22:23; Acts 23:8). They believed that the soul did not exist after death. Josephus says that they "take away the belief of the immortal duration of the soul, and the punishments and rewards in Hades".[2] They taught that the soul dies with the body. According to the Talmudic writers, they denied that there was any other world than this. It seems strange that they should deny that there were angels because in the five books of Moses mention is made frequently of angels but it seems that they understood those allegorically, or as apparitions caused by God to reveal his mind unto men. It is said that their teaching of no resurrection had its rise in the thought that God's servants should not do service with the hope of reward as the life to come would be a reward by itself.[3] They deny the existence of any spiritual beings distinct from God himself and their rejection of resurrection (Acts 23:8) obviously contradicts the prophecy of Daniel and teaching of Jesus Christ (cf. Dan. 12:2; John 11:25). Jesus Christ, the Son of Man, has authority to raise the dead buried in 'the dust of the earth' to a personal resurrection or to condemnation according to the will of the God the Father (John 5:27–30).

EPICUREAN AND STOIC PHILOSOPHERS

Another challenge to the doctrine of the resurrection in the New Testament times came from the Athenian philosophers (Acts 17). Paul addressed the gathered crowd in the midst of the Areopagus (Mars Hill). In his concluding speech he proclaiming that Jesus ('the Man') ordained by God was to rise from the dead. This was somewhat ground-breaking for those who heard him and the narrative tells us that after the crowd broke up some mocked but others were willing to listen again later on (vv. 32–34). The Epicureans, take their name from their founder (BC 341–270) who taught that the world was created by chance, and they mocked popular mythology. Their view of the soul was similar to that of the Sadducees, viz. it was materialistic and denied immortality. This philosophical view is also held by various religious cults today (see below) but unlike the cults, who teach adherence to the Ten

Commandments, the Epicureans were hedonistic and were not regulated by high moral or spiritual interests. Virtue for them was prudence in pleasure. They were guided by reason, indifferent to pleasure, pain and to suffering while regarding themselves self-sufficient. Human pride was their besetting sin. Their philosophy was diametrically opposed to Paul's gospel and his doctrine of God and redemption through Jesus Christ, especially the resurrection of the body and victory over the last enemy death. They called Paul 'this seedpicker' (*spermologos*) implying arrogantly that he was unlearned and was chattering about the bits and pieces he had picked up here and there (v. 18).[4] Thus he was not to be taken seriously. However, we read that all was not lost when, 'some men joined him and believed, among them Dionysius the Areopagite, a woman named Damaris, and others with them' (Acts 17:34). Paul under the guidance of the Holy Spirit called his Athenian listeners away from ignorance and idolatry to faith in the resurrection of Jesus (vv. 29–31). The resurrection of Jesus Christ is a sign and also a warning of the judgement yet to come, so it is a call to repentance; 'God … now commands all men everywhere to repent' (v. 30).

HYMENAEUS AND PHILETUS

Two opponents of biblical resurrection are found in the New Testament: their names are Hymenaeus and Philetus. Paul calls their opposition to the resurrection 'profane *and* idle babblings' and says to his readers that they 'have strayed concerning the truth, saying that the resurrection is already past; and they overthrow the faith of some' (2 Tim. 2:17–18). This later phrase 'they overthrow the faith of some' highlights how important this doctrine is and that it must be embraced by faith. William Hendriksen summarises their error:

- They were teachers of heresy.
- Hymenaeus was probably the leader and is associated also with

Alexander (1 Tim. 1:19, 20). We know nothing else about Philetus ('beloved') but his name.

- They had wandered away from the truth.
- They claimed that 'the resurrection is already past' and denied the resurrection of the body, as do some present-day liberal theologians (cf., 1 Cor. 15; Phil. 3:21).
- What made matters worse was that Hymenaeus and Philetus professed to be Christians. From 1 Timothy 1:20 it appears that they were excommunicated.
- Their false teaching ('incipient gnosticism') was contagious and 'overthrew the faith of some'.[5]

2. Support

Jewish theology and Gentile philosophy failed to understand what had been revealed in God's dealings with Israel and recorded in the Scriptures giving a clear reference to the soul's existence after death and the hope of resurrection. This can be found in 1 Kings 17. There Elijah, the famous prophet, was called on one occasion to raise a dead child of a widow in Zarephath through powerful intercession (v. 17). Elijah looked to God 'and cried out to the Lord'. In the case of true prophets the power to heal or raise up is conditional on fervent prayer: 'And he stretched himself out on the child three times, and cried out to the Lord and said, "O Lord my God, I pray, let this child's soul come back to him." Then the Lord heard the voice of Elijah; and the soul of the child came back to him, and he revived' (vv. 21–22).

Matthew Henry commenting says, 'Elijah's prayer was doubtless directed by the Holy Spirit and the child revived. See the power of prayer, and the power of Him who hears prayer.'[6] This miracle, though wrought by God alone, is in answer to believing prayer (cf. Acts 20:10; James 5:16). Elijah's petition, 'Let this child's soul come into him again' makes it clear that the soul was gone out of his body and therefore does exist after death' (cf. Gen. 35:18 and the death of Rachel).

BOOK OF DANIEL

'Sleep' in the Book of Daniel (12:2) is a euphemism for death (cf., John 11:11; Acts 7:60; 1 Thess. 4:14, 5:10) and the context illustrates the same point; 'in the dust of the earth' is figurative of the grave: Calvin says, 'Literally ... meaning those who are reduced to earth and dust.'[7] However, some commentators see verse 2 as referring *not* to physical resurrection but to the national and moral revival of Israel:

Many of those who sleep in the dust of the earth shall awake, some to everlasting life, some to shame *and* everlasting contempt.

Personal resurrection is indicated in as, 'many ... shall *awake*' (cf. Isa. 29:19). Those who awake to 'everlasting contempt' (Heb. *shame*) are lost forever while, 'Those who are wise shall shine like the brightness of the firmament, and those who turn many to righteousness like the stars forever and ever' (Dan. 12:3). This prophecy speaks of the resurrection of the righteous believers and is not pertinent to a fallen and sinful nation as Israel (John 5:25, cf. Matt. 13:43; 1 Cor. 15:40ff; Rev. 2:28).

WORDS OF JESUS

In one incident the Sadducees clashed with Jesus on this topic (Matt. 22:33; Mark 12:18–27; Luke 20:27–40). They approached Jesus with a 'what if' question, designed to show that they conjectured and imagined that absurd consequences can arise from believing in the immortality of the soul and resurrection of the dead. Suppose, they asked, a woman had seven husbands and each of them died without leaving children, whose wife would she be in the world to come? Jesus replied with a two-part answer. Firstly, he said that they were wrong to suggest that earthly relationships, such as marriage, will continue after the resurrection: 'in the resurrection they neither marry nor are given in marriage, but are like angels of God in heaven' (Matt. 22:30). Secondly, Jesus pointed out that they were wrong in not believing in a resurrection: 'concerning the resurrection of the dead, have you not read what was spoken to you by God, saying, I am the God of Abraham, the God of Isaac, and the God of Jacob? God is not the God of the dead, but of the living' (vv. 31–32). The Sadducees sought their authority in the written law of Moses but Jesus's argument was that despite all their learning they were 'mistaken, not knowing the Scriptures nor the power of God' (v. 29). God told Moses that He (Jehovah) was the God of Abraham, Isaac and Jacob; for God is not the God of the dead but of the living, therefore it is wrong to deny life after death and the resurrection of the dead.

SAUL THE PHARISEE

As we meet the Pharisees (*separated ones*) in the New Testament, they are mainly members of the priestly order, and were ordinary people. They were known for insisting that the law of God be observed as the scribes interpreted it and also for their special commitment to keeping the laws of tithing and ritual purity. The Pharisees spelled out and endorsed the meaning of the Mosaic Law and their time-honoured customs became a part of the tradition of the elders (Mark 7:3). The Pharisees believed it was important to observe all the laws of God, which they taught and were as many as 613. Pharisees observed the law carefully as far as appearances went, but their hearts were far from God (Matt. 6:2, 5, 16; 23:57). They also had evil desires that were hidden by their outward demonstration of piety (Matt. 23:25). That is why Pharisees were often called hypocrites (Matt. 15:7–9). The Pharisees thought they could match God's standards by keeping all the outward rules. Jesus told the people that their clergy trusted in themselves and thought that they were righteous, but he taught that God would provide a better righteousness:

I say to you, that unless your righteousness exceeds the righteousness of the scribes and Pharisees, you will by no means enter the kingdom of heaven. (Matt. 5:20)

The Pharisees believed in the resurrection of the dead. This is made clear by Paul's reply when being interrogated by the Sanhedrin in Jerusalem, 'I am a Pharisee, the son of a Pharisee; concerning the hope and resurrection of the dead I am being judged!' However, 'when he had said this, a dissension arose between the Pharisees and the Sadducees; and the assembly was divided' (Acts 23:6–7). From this passage, we see that Paul, as a Pharisee, held to the hope of the resurrection. This was the ancient faith of Israel (see Chart 7). Paul also knew personally that Jesus was alive because of his own encounter with him on the Damascus Road:

I fell to the ground and heard a voice saying to me, 'Saul, Saul, why are you persecuting Me?' So I answered, 'Who are You, Lord?' And He said to me, 'I am Jesus of Nazareth, whom you are persecuting.' (Acts 22:7–8)[8]

And the Lord said to me, 'Arise and go into Damascus, and there you will be told all things which are appointed for you to do.' (Acts 22:10)

I was in a trance and saw Him saying to me, 'Make haste and get out of Jerusalem quickly.' (Acts 22:17, 18)

THE ACTS

Paul's declaration on the Sabbath day to the assembled group at the synagogue in Antioch in Pisidia was about the third day bodily resurrection of Jesus. He wanted to make it clear that Jesus's resurrection was distinct and separate from the other recorded 'resurrections', in Scripture, such as the widow of Zarephath's son (1 Kgs. 17), the widow of Nain's son (Luke 7:14–15), Jairus's young daughter (Luke 8:56–57) and those who came out of their tombs the time of his death on the cross (Matt. 27:52–53; see Appendix 3), so Paul says:

God raised Him from the dead. He was seen for many days by those who came up with Him from Galilee to Jerusalem, who are His witnesses to the people … And that He raised Him from the dead, no more to return to corruption. (Acts 13:28, 31, 33b, 34)

This last phrase *'no more to return to corruption'* draws attention to something new, something unknown and unexpected. In verse 35 the Apostle quotes from Psalm 16:10, 'You will not allow Your Holy One to see corruption', and with this Paul was telling them that since the Lord Jesus rose from the dead, death had no more power over Him. He will never die again, nor will his body see corruption (decay). David in Psalm 16 could not have been speaking about himself. The Lord Jesus was raised from the dead three days after He died. What a message to hear; what a fact to consider; what a doctrine to receive; what an event to believe! Its heralding was unique to this synagogue and to all in Asia Minor too! King David (Paul said), 'was buried with his fathers, and saw corruption; but He whom God raised up saw no corruption' (Acts 13:36–37). Resurrection was now on the table! It was now a fact to be reckoned with, a truth to be accepted and a hope to be embraced (by faith).

In Acts 23:6 in a debate with the Sadducees, Paul witnessed to his faith, 'Men *and* brethren, I am a Pharisee, the son of a Pharisee; concerning the hope and resurrection of the dead I am being judged.' This hope led Paul to write a defence of bodily resurrection in 1 Corinthians chapter 15. In the later verses of that chapter, under the inspiration of the Spirit of God, he speaks of the resurrection and the (future) glory it provides for us. Through His resurrection Jesus Christ became a 'life giving spirit' (v. 45), i.e. the 'fountain of spiritual life for us' and at the resurrection day the Holy Spirit will take complete control of the body. As Lenski says, the 'first man is about the body but the second man is about the person'.[9] Before Adam fell his body was not ready for immortal existence but at the resurrection things are different. Adam was given life but Christ *is* Life and has life in Himself (John 5:26). Jesus Christ *is* the second man and is of a higher order than the first Adam.

PETER THE APOSTLE

The apostles after Pentecost (being filled with the Holy Spirit) were emboldened by the truth of the resurrection from the dead of Jesus their friend and Saviour whom they called the Christ having personally witnessed this miracle and embraced its reality and implications (John 1:14). When Peter preached on the Day of Pentecost (Acts 2) he quotes from the Book of Psalms that the Messiah's resurrection had been foretold, 'You will not leave my soul in Sheol, nor will You allow Your Holy One to see corruption' (Acts 2:27; Ps. 16:10). Peter, having spoken first about Jesus's ministry of 'miracles, wonders and signs' (Acts 2:22), and Jesus's cruel death by crucifixion, announced that God raised him up, 'God raised up, having loosed the pains of death' (v. 24) all in fulfilment of Old Testament Scripture. Jesus Christ—the descendent of King David in the flesh—was predicted to 'be raised up' to sit on David's throne (cf. 2 Sam. 7:12). However, as a prophet, David looked forward in the Spirit to the resurrection of the Messiah (v. 30). Jesus was not left in death nor did His body see corruption. Peter in his sermon wanted to establish the fact that Jesus is the promised Messiah:

[David], foreseeing ... the resurrection of the Christ, that His soul was not left in Hades, nor did His flesh see corruption. This Jesus God has raised up, of which we are all witnesses. (Acts 2:31)[10]

Peter also quoted from Psalm 132, 'The Lord has sworn *in* truth to David; He will not turn from it: "I will set upon your throne the fruit of your body"' (Ps. 132:11) and he assured them that this was no hoax or prank: 'This Jesus God has raised up, of which we are all witnesses' (v. 32).

In Acts 3, Peter and John, on their way into the temple, performed a miracle of healing on a 'man lame from his mother's womb' (3:2) but made it clear that it was not *they* but faith in Jesus, whom God raised from the dead, 'that gave him his perfect soundness in the presence of you all' (vv. 13–16). Old Testament prophecy and New Testament reality formed the basis of Peter's sermon and faith as he emphasised his eyewitness credentials (3:15). It is interesting to note that Peter twice stated, 'God raised Jesus from the dead ... to bless you' (vv. 15, 28). However, Peter and John were arrested and interrogated by the Sadducees who were 'greatly disturbed' when they heard them preaching the story of Jesus and his resurrection from the dead with great success in the temple precincts (4:2, 4). They were accused of subversion and insurrection—very grave charges—and so spent the night in custody before being examined (4:3). The next day Peter's defence in a sermon was delivered to the 'rulers, elders, and scribes, as well as Annas the high priest, Caiaphas, John, and Alexander, and as many as were of the family of the high priest, were gathered together at Jerusalem' (v. 6), saying:

Let it be known to you all, and to all the people of Israel, that by the name of Jesus Christ of Nazareth, whom you crucified, whom *God raised from the dead*, by Him this man stands here before you whole. (Acts 4:8–10)

Of course the Sadducees had heard enough of this doctrine of resurrection which they rejected utterly as impossible. These words were spoken by the same fisherman who had previously denied he knew Jesus (John 18:15–17) but now filled with resurrection hope spoke without fear in the presence of the learned company. Peter went on to repeat his belief in the resurrection again in Acts 10 when we find him preaching to Cornelius and his household. His sermon was similar to that in Acts 4 where he spoke again of the promised Messiah's mission to save while emphasising Jesus's miraculous resurrection from the dead:

Him God raised up on the third day, and showed Him openly, not to all the people, but to witnesses chosen before by God, *even* to us who ate and drank with Him after *He arose from the dead.* (10:40–41)

God, *through the resurrection of Jesus Christ'*, has brought salvation to all who will believe. (10:43)

Three things are emphasised: (i) the 'third day'; (ii) the providing of credible and honest witnesses by God to the fact of the resurrection; and (iii) faith in the gospel story is essential to the forgiveness of sins. The inclusion by Peter of the 'third day' registers the event as historical and a fulfilment of Jesus own prophecy:

Destroy this temple, and in three days I will raise it up. (John 2:18–19)

SIGNS AND WONDERS

The Jews were looking for a sign of legitimisation to Jesus's claims to be the Son of God. They wanted to see miracles; they wanted Jesus to authenticate his ministry with signs and wonders so His claim as a Prophet of God and Reformer of Israel was recognised. This desire of the Jews was a constant theme throughout Christ's ministry (Matt. 12:38–39; 16:1–4; Luke 11:29–30). It had its roots in their history, because every prophet of renown was able to prove by works of power that God was with him (Moses, Elijah, Elisha, etc.). Moses said that the true Messiah would be recognised by His words of fulfilled prophecy (Deut. 18:15–22).

In Matthew 12:39–40 Jesus offered the Pharisees the sign of the prophet Jonah: 'An evil and adulterous generation seeks after a sign, and no sign will be given to it except the sign of the prophet Jonah.' As Jonah was three days and three nights in the belly of the great fish, so Jesus will be three days and three nights in the heart of the earth (Matt. 12:39–40). The sign is about the time Jonah spent in the belly of the great fish. It typified Jesus's three days in the tomb. The resurrection of Jesus from the dead was a sign to the world that Jesus Christ is the Lord of glory but will they believe it? The chosen witnesses were alive and willing to both speak and talk if asked (Acts 2:24–32; cf. 1 Cor. 15:6). From the Day of Pentecost Peter preached that God raised Jesus Christ up on the third day and called for faith bringing salvation:

Blessed *be* the God and Father of our Lord Jesus Christ, who according to His abundant mercy has begotten us again to a living hope through the resurrection of Jesus Christ from the dead. (1 Pet. 1:3)

NOTES

1 Tony Sergent, *Gems from Martyn Lloyd-Jones* (Milton Keynes: Paternoster, 2007), p. 252.

2 Josephus, *Jewish Wars*, Book ii, Chapter 8, Section 14.

3 Help was received from: https://biblehub.com/commentaries/acts/23-8.html

4 R C H Lenski, *The Acts of the Apostles* (Minneapolis, MI: Augsburg Publishing House, 1961), p. 715.

5 William Hendriksen, *1 & 2 Timothy and Titus* (Edinburgh: The Banner of Truth Trust, 1972), pp. 264–266.

6 Matthew Henry, *Commentary on the Whole Bible*, Vol. 2 (London: Pickering and Inglis Ltd, c. 1972).

7 John Calvin, *Daniel* (Edinburgh: The Banner of Truth, 1986), p. 373.

8 Remember that the Sadducees did not believe. They denied the existence of any spiritual beings distinct from God himself and the possibility of resurrection. They rejected Paul's understanding of Abraham's trial of faith in Genesis 22 when God asks Abraham to sacrifice his son, Isaac, on Mt Moriah (Heb. 11:17–19; cf. Gen. 22).

9 Lenski, *1 & 2 Corinthians*, pp. 772–773, 725.

10 Here is the only New Testament description of David as a prophet (Acts 2:30).

The intermediate state

Calvin taught that for believers the intermediate state is one of both blessedness and expectation—the blessedness is therefore provisional and incomplete. (A A Hoekema)[1]

Hold on to the doctrine of the resurrection of the body. We shall not spend our eternity as disembodied spirits. (Dr Martyn Lloyd-Jones)[2]

The resurrection of the body is taught clearly in Scripture and is plain to all that will receive it (John 11; 1 Corinthians 15). However, there are two distinctions to be made when one thinks on the Christian view of eternal life: the first is what can be called the *intermediate state*. This is a disembodied state when the soul/spirit is separated from the body by death (Acts 7:59).[3] The second distinction is the *resurrection state*. Thus, when one thinks about life after death one needs then to think about the distinction that the Bible makes between (i) disembodied spirits and (ii) resurrected bodies. The former follows death and the latter follows the general resurrection. One is existence in a celestial state and the other in the resurrected body. The first is the heaven of 'just men made perfect' (Heb. 12:23), the second is the 'new heavens and the new earth' (Rev. 21:1).

The intermediate state

To understand the path God has for humanity we need to grasp that the New Testament teaches three states of being which make up the whole of an individual's existence. Firstly, the *temporal state* which is the life in the body we have now. Secondly, the *intermediate state*, i.e. life in heaven with Christ immediately after death. Thirdly, the *eternal state* when believers enjoy eternal life in the new heavens and new earth with resurrection bodies resembling that of the resurrected Christ. Thus, while in heaven now, deceased believers are with God awaiting the resurrection day and the fulfilment of gospel promises (1 Thess. 3:13; 4:16). Life after death in heaven for the believer is a temporary state.

Where are the dead who die 'in Christ' now? We answer, they are in heaven because Scriptures teach that to be absent from the body is to be present ('at home') with the Lord (2 Cor. 5:8; Phil. 1:21f). This is the same heavenly place that Jesus our Lord promised to the thief on the cross the day he died (Luke 23:43). The present condition of those who died in Christ is blessed and their state glorious and they are conscious and awake as well as happy and holy. Yes, they are bereft of a bodily existence as we have now and it is not their final state. In heaven they are not yet in possession of their full reward, which along with heaven has been promised to them as an inheritance (1 Pet. 1:3–4). Those asleep in the grave now are waiting the resurrection day, when all will arise from the dead (John 5:28, 29). There is also the promise of the new heavens and the new earth yet to come.

In heaven the redeemed souls await the Second Advent when they will take possession of their promised inheritance and be given their reward (Phil. 3:20; 1 Thess. 3:13; 4:14–18; Rom. 8:19–23; 2 Peter 3:10–13; and Rev. 21:1–4). Thus the intermediate state is that realm in which souls exist between death and the resurrection until the last day. Those redeemed, 'sleep' in the intermediate state of blessedness with all the spirits of the church militant in heaven awaiting Christ's Second Coming. They are the 'Spirits of just men made perfect' (Rev. 21:23). We are to look forward to this great and wonderful day. It is great and also terrible, as it is also the Judgement Day.

Jesus Christ and Lazarus (John 11)

As we have seen above Martha (Lazarus' sister), with her contemporaries, believed in the future resurrection of the righteous on the last day. This is the witness of the Old Testament (Job 19:25–26; Dan. 12:2, 3; see Chart 5). Martha is happy with Jesus's statement (v. 23) and she replies, 'I know that he will rise again in the resurrection at the last day.' In His response Jesus discloses not only that He is in *Himself* the power of resurrection but that He too believes in the future resurrection state:

I am the resurrection and the life. He who believes in Me, though he may die, he shall live. (v. 25)

Jesus's view of his own destiny is clear (John 2:18–22; 3:15; 4:10; 5:28; 13:30, 43) and His declaration as the Redeemer of the body was made clear to Martha. Jesus spoke these words to her giving her present hope and future expectation. Soon her brother Lazarus will, by a miracle, rise from 'sleep' (v. 11, i.e. death) even though his corpse had been in the grave four days (v. 17). Jesus also promised a future salvation that is of endless life gained by faith (alone) in Him:

And whoever lives and believes in Me shall never die. Do you believe this? (v. 26)

These words of Jesus Christ are the most amazing that any man or woman has ever uttered or heard. They take us to the heart of the gospel and they challenge us to believe something utterly astounding and wholly unexpected. Who is *this* person who says, if you 'believe in Me you shall never die'? No one else in all history has dared to say anything like it! Yet, this man did. We must grasp His greatness and the import of the statement as He spoke to Lazarus' sisters. Has anyone in the history of the world also made this claim? Has any other? A pope of Rome, or Patriarch, Archbishop or Hindu guru? Who would dare? Yet Jesus son of Mary, Son of God has, and on the evidence of His own resurrection laid down a challenge to all who read His-story. We should take heed to His words and the promise they bring.

Purgatory[4]

It is necessary in this chapter to make mention of the Roman Catholic (RC) doctrine of Purgatory as it impinges on the topic of the *intermediate state* in a big way.[5] The doctrine is not found in the Bible, but RC theologians reckon that it does. One RC web site states:

- 'The Catechism of the Catholic Church defines purgatory as a "purification, so as to achieve the holiness necessary to enter the joy of heaven" which is experienced by those "who die in God's grace and friendship, but still imperfectly purified"' (CCC 1030). It notes that 'this final purification of the elect … is entirely different from the punishment of the damned' (CCC 1031).
- 'The purification is necessary because, as Scripture teaches, nothing unclean will enter the presence of God in heaven (Rev. 21:27) and, while we may die with our mortal sins forgiven, there can still be many impurities in us, specifically *venial sins* and the temporal punishment due to sins already forgiven.'
- 'When we die, we undergo what is called the particular, or individual, judgment. Scripture says that "it is appointed for men to die once, and after that comes judgment" (Heb. 9:27). We are judged instantly and receive our reward, for good or ill. We know at once what our final destiny will be. At the end of time, when Jesus returns, there will come the general judgement to which the Bible refers, for example, in Matthew 25:31-32: "When the Son of man comes in his glory, and all the angels with him, then he will sit on his glorious throne. Before him will be gathered all the nations, and he will separate them one from another as a shepherd separates the sheep from the goats." In this general judgement all our sins will be publicly revealed' (Luke 12:2–5).[6]

The post (quoted above) has used Bible reference out of context thus giving the impression to unaware readers that there is biblical warrant for this dogma. However, in the blog post there is hidden context:

- What is said presupposes baptismal regeneration and the sanctification of the Catholic faithful through masses and the other sacraments of Rome. If future 'purification' by fire is required for RCs this shows impotence in their religion and beliefs! The Bible teaches free grace and not 'good' works or papal magic (Eph. 2:8–9).
- To say that those 'who die in God's grace and friendship, but still imperfectly purified', points to the sacraments of Holy Unction and Confession. The priesthood of Rome is the key here but the Bible say we are to pray for ourselves in the name of Jesus claiming the priesthood of all believers (Acts 9:11; Matt. 6:12).[7]
- To say as above, 'We know at once what our final destiny will be' is misleading as it seems to fix a RC's destiny, yet the policy of Rome is to pray the soul out of purgatory before the final Judgement Day (cf. Rom. 6:23). However, beatification changes this 'final destiny' and masses said and prayers made are to shorten the event for a few!
- No definition is given of 'the dammed' as it is stated the RC Church will get their people into heaven eventually. But there are, 'children of the devil' as well as 'children of God' (John 8:44; 1 John 3:10). Rome claims that it is able to save all its baptised children but this contradicts the doctrine of election as well as justification by faith only (Matt. 22:14; Rom. 5:1; 9:6–13; Eph. 1:3–14; 1 Peter 1:2).
- To say, 'We are judged instantly and receive our reward, for good or ill' is misleading as the rewards are inseparable from the resurrection and are not found in the fires of torment. The RC doctrine is unclear here (2 Cor. 5:8; Matt. 25:13).
- The scheme described above is a devised and substituted alternative for true, 'Godly sorrow' aided by the Holy Spirit of God, unto salvation, the sacrament of penance brings a false assurance of peace and salvation (2 Cor. 7:10).

• Our prayers can add nothing to the destiny of the dead in hell
when we rightly understand that it 'is appointed for men to die
once, but after this the judgment' (Heb. 9:27).

Purgatory is the false alternative to the *intermediate state* in RC
theology. RC members are told they will be made fit for heaven through a
process of fire purification in purgatory. It entails various spans of time
and much pain not unlike that of hell. Hell is only of greater duration!
Historically it found its beginning in Origen of Alexandria and was
meant to give hope to sinners with the aim of fitting them for heaven.
Theologically, those who sin after baptism were made the subjects of
prayer and masses to aid their purifying, even the popes. Religiously, it is
all those baptised by Rome and who die in the grace of the Church of
Rome, are promised purgatory.[8] Under Rome's teaching purgatory will
eventually be empty.

Suffering in purgatory can be shortened 'by gifts of money, prayers by
priests, and masses, which gifts, prayers, and masses can be provided for by
the person before death or relatives or friends after death'.[9] This practice is
not sound in logic nor is it just as it makes God a respecter of persons and
favourable to the rich and unfavourable to the poor. Neither does Old or
New Testaments sanction its practice. Not one prayer for the dead is found
in the Scriptures. The doctrine of purgatory is taken from the Apocrypha
and 2 Maccabees where verses are said to refer to prayers that will help the
deceased. Those departed in the fires of purgatory can do nothing to help
themselves and are dependent only on rescue through the prayers of their
fellows: what a fearful prospect!

Prayers for the dead

Intercessions and petitions for the deceased in purgatory are predicated
on the idea that the state of the Christian dead is not fixed and that it can
be changed or improved with human intervention or why would money
be exchanged or masses said on the dead's behalf? This practice is

contrary to the doctrines of Scripture. It also suggests that human prayers have a greater power than those of the risen and ascended Jesus Christ 'whoever lives to make intercession for us'! If prayer for those for whom Jesus Christ died is an urgent necessity why does the 'sacred heart' of Jesus Christ not pray for them? Surely one prayer of the Saviour would be enough to whisk a soul from purgatory into heaven (1 John 2:1, 2)? For Rome, the idea of punishment and atonement taking place in the afterlife is a second atonement made by baptised RCs to save themselves. The Westminster Confession of Faith on this topic states:

Prayer is to be made for things lawful, and for all sorts of men living, or that shall live hereafter; *but not for the dead*, nor for those of whom it may be known that they have sinned the sin unto death.[10]

A (suggested) prayer of the dead is said to be: 'Father of all, we pray to you for N., and for all those whom we love but see no longer. Grant to them eternal rest. Let light perpetual shine upon them. May his soul and the souls of all the departed, through the mercy of God, rest in peace.'[11] This request surely is a contradiction to the process of sanctification of the soul and its 'purification, to achieve the holiness necessary to enter the joy of heaven'! Supposed support is found by RCs in 2 Timothy which speaks of Onesiphorus, 'the Lord grant to him that he may find mercy from the Lord in that Day'. This verse is misused by Roman Catholic theologians to support prayers for the dead. The argument is that Onesiphorus had already died when Paul wrote this and that Paul was asking God to show mercy to him. However, it is not at all clear that Onesiphorus was dead; Paul only refers to him in the past tense. Was Onesiphorus dead is the issue here? It is conjecture and concluded that he was by Rome, but even if so, it is unwise to propagate a dogma on such uncertain proof: 'There is not the vaguest hint that Onesiphorus was dead. Proponents of this view are idle babblers clutching at a straw to shore up an unbiblical practice.'[12] Some prefer to think that Onesiphorus had forsaken Paul along with others at some point and that is why the Apostle prays, 'The Lord grant to him that he may find mercy from the Lord in that Day', i.e. by restoring him from his association with Phygellus and Hermogenes and his backsliding. Paul was obviously grateful to him and his household for past support:

The Lord grant mercy to the household of Onesiphorus, for he often refreshed me, and was not ashamed of my chain; but when he arrived in Rome, he sought me out very zealously and found me. (2 Tim. 1:15–18)

The way of salvation

Following Calvin, the Reformed Protestant Confessions and theologians teach the doctrine of the intermediate state and although some in the last century have questioned Calvin's view, it remains the orthodox position. As Hoekema says, 'there is enough biblical evidence to enable us to maintain that at death man is not annihilated and the believer is not separated from Christ'.[13] The Westminster Shorter Catechism Q. 37 sets forth this theology:

Q. What benefits do the believers receive from Christ at death?
A. The souls of believers are at death made perfect in holiness, and do immediately pass into glory; and their bodies, being still united to Christ, do rest in their grave till the resurrection.

This teaching offers saved persons peace with assurance and recommends an anchor of hope 'both sure and steadfast':

We … who have fled for refuge lay hold of the hope set before *us*. This *hope* we have as an anchor of the soul, both sure and steadfast, and which enters the Presence *behind* the veil, where the forerunner has entered for us, *even* Jesus's. (Heb. 6:18b–20a)

Chapter 7

It is of course true that nothing that would defile heaven will be allowed to enter. It is a holy place and it is holy beyond our imagination (Isa. 6:1ff; Ezek.1:1ff; Acts 3:21; 1 Cor. 15:47; Rev. 19:1; 20:1; 21:2) therefore the Westminster Larger Catechism Q. 86, states, 'The communion in glory with Christ, which the members of the invisible church enjoy immediately after death, is, in that their souls are then made perfect in holiness' (Heb. 12:23). Such faith allows us to die like one of old, 'Yes; tell them I died in the faith—*full in the faith.*'[14] Jesus came and died and rose again the third day so that we are be made holy and regain the communion with God that was lost at the Fall in Eden. Protestants reject the RC way of salvation through their programme of seven sacraments, good deeds and via imagined purgatory.[15] There would be no need of a purgatory if salvation was sought by grace alone, through faith alone, in Christ alone (Eph. 2:8–10). C H Spurgeon, thinking on God's heavenly Paradise illustrated in the Old Testament (Zech. 6:13), sees no place for purgatory:

Christ himself is the builder of his spiritual temple, and he has built it on the mountains of his unchangeable affection, his omnipotent grace, and his infallible truthfulness. But as it was in Solomon's temple, so in this; the materials need making ready. There are the rough stones still in the quarry, they must be hewn thence, and squared. All this is Christ's own work. Each individual believer is being prepared, and polished, and made ready for his place in the temple; but Christ's own hand performs the preparation-work. Afflictions cannot sanctify, excepting as they are used by him to this end. Our prayers and efforts cannot make us ready for heaven, apart from the hand of Jesus, who fashioned our hearts aright. As in the building of Solomon's temple, 'there was neither hammer, nor axe, nor any tool of iron, heard in the house,' so is it with the temple which Jesus builds; the making ready is all done on earth. When we reach heaven, there will be no sanctifying us there, no squaring us with affliction, no planing us with suffering. No, we must be made meet here—all *that* Christ will do beforehand; and when he has done it, we shall be ferried by a loving hand across the stream of death, and brought to the heavenly Jerusalem, to abide as eternal pillars in the temple of our Lord.[16]

Conclusion

Where are the dead who die in Christ? They are in heaven for the Holy Scriptures teach that to be absent from the body is to be present with the Lord (2 Cor. 5:8). This is the same heaven that Jesus our Lord promised to the thief on the cross when he died believing him to be the Jewish Messiah/Christ (Luke 23:43). Those in the heaven now await the resurrection day, when all men will arise from the dead and receive their reward (John 5:28–29).

The present condition of those who died in Christ is blessedly glorious. However, they are limited to heaven and are not yet in possession of the earth, which along with heaven has been promised to them as an inheritance (cf. 1 Peter 1:3–4). Now, they are bereft of a body, and this bodiless existence is not their final resting place.[17] In heaven the redeemed await the coming 'shout' from the Son of God at his Second Coming when He will bring the redeemed disembodied spirits with Him as He returns to earth. Until then we await that day (the Day of the Lord) when the saved will take possession of their promised inheritance and be given their rewards (1 Thess. 3:13; 4:14–18; 1 Peter 1:3–4). Can you sing with the author?

When my life's work is ended and I cross the swelling tide,
    When the bright and glorious morning I shall see;
I shall know my Redeemer when I reach the other side,
    And His smile will be the first to welcome me.

Through the gates of the city in a robe of spotless white,
    He will lead me where no tears shall ever fall;

Chapter 7

In the glad song of ages I shall mingle with delight,

But I long to meet my Saviour first of all.

I shall know Him, I shall know Him,

As redeemed by His side I shall stand.

I shall know Him, I shall know Him,

By the prints of the nails in His hands.

(Fanny J Crosby)

NOTES

1 A A Hoekema, *The Bible and the Future* (Exeter: The Paternoster Press, 1979), p. 92.

2 Sergent, *Gems*, p. 253.

3 The Scriptures teach that man is a unity and that 'body and soul' (Matt. 10:28) or 'body and spirit' (1 Cor. 7:43; James 2:26) belong together.

4 For a discussion of the Roman Catholic doctrines of *Limbus Patrum* and *Limbus Infantum*, see Loraine Boettner, *Immortality* (Philadelphia, Pe: P&R Publishing, 1979), pp. 102–104.

5 'The Greeks [Orthodox] rejected the idea of punishment and atonement taking place in the afterlife, yet they shared with the [RC] church in the West the practice of interceding for the dead by prayer, alms, good works, and, most notably, the offering of the Eucharist [Requiem Masses] for their repose.' See, Joseph Ratzinger, *Eschatology* (Washington D.C: CU of AP, 1988), p. 219.

6 https://www.catholic.com/tract/purgatory The word *purgatory* is not found in Scripture nor is the doctrine.

7 See my book, *Getting to Grips with Prayer* (Day One, 2017), pp. 57–61.

8 All who commit mortal sins go immediately to hell.

9 Boettner, *Immortality*, p. 126.

10 See John 5:14; 17:20; 1 Tim. 2:1–2; Luke 16:25–26; 1 John 5:16; Rev. 5:16. Emphasis mine. See *The Wesminster Confession of Faith*, chapter 21, 'Of Religious Worship', and the Sabbath Day, Para. 4.

11 https://en.wikipedia.org/wiki/Prayer_for_the_dead

12 Jowett quoted in *Believers Bible Commentary*, Nelson CD_ROM.

13 Hoekema, *The Bible*, p. 94.

14 Quoted in John Whitecross, *The Shorter Catechism Illustrated* (London: The Banner of Truth

Trust, *c.* 1994), p. 62.

15 The Roman Catholic sacraments are understood as, 'visible rites seen as signs and efficacious channels of the grace of God to all those who receive them with the proper disposition. Their order of importance is; Baptism, Confirmation, Holy Communion, Confession, Marriage, Holy Orders, and the Anointing of the Sick.' https://www.google.com/search?q=seven+sacraments+of+the+catholic+church&rlz=1C1CHBF_

16 C H Spurgeon, *Morning & Evening* (McLean, VA: MacDonald Publishing, *c.* 1980), June 22.

17 Dr H Bavinck in A A Hoekema, *The Bible and the Future*, pp. 58ff

The Resurrection: Its blessings

I am the resurrection and the life. He who believes in Me, though he may die, he shall live. And whoever lives and believes in Me shall never die. Do you believe this? (John 11:25–26)

There are great and blessed consequences because of Jesus Christ's resurrection victory both cosmic and spiritual. The founder of Christianity was unique and we can therefore expect uniqueness in all His graces and from all His works and in the blessings which flow from His resurrection victory.

After 2,000 years Jesus Christ is still loved and served and worshipped as God incarnate who came to save us. To some this is myth and to others it is blasphemy but, to all those who believe, it is the gospel and the power of God unto salvation (Rom. 1:16). His story is history (true and transparent) and this is why it is to be believed. He came to bring us back to God from the dark paths of sin. The story of the Christ has God's divine blessing on it and we are invited to believe on Jesus Christ as our personal Saviour, the 'way' to God and heaven (John 14:6).

The gift of salvation through the power of the atoning sacrifice of Jesus Christ's cross brings forgiveness and sweet peace to the soul. It is found when one seeks the grace of God personally through repentant prayer and justifying faith. Salvation's blessings and benefits are many flowing from God's free grace because of the resurrection:

Firstly, the devil is defeated: Jesus Christ's story is still told so that no one is left in dark about the reality that is *Love* and *Light* and *Life*. The defeat of Satan and the justification of believing sinners are prominent themes in the New Testament. In Colossians we read that Christ 'disarmed principalities and powers':

Having wiped out the handwriting of requirements that was against us, which was contrary to us. And He has taken it out of the way, having nailed it to the cross. Having disarmed principalities and powers, He made a public spectacle of them, triumphing over them in it. (Col. 2:14–15)

Satan and his forces were dealt a powerful and lethal blow of defeat at Calvary. These dark powers gathered against Jesus as He hung on the cross. So the Bible speaks of the resurrection of Christ as a great victory when He broke the chains of death and hell and by His resurrection He made *captivity captive*, displaying to the whole of creation that He is Lord (Eph. 4:8). Many think that Paul is using the imagery of a Roman victory parade saying, 'he made a public spectacle of them', such as when Rome's Imperial army marched in procession with their captives chained behind them as trophies before the citizens of Rome. Christ has defeated Satan who had the power of death. This power was taken from Him at the cross (Heb. 2:14–15). He is not 'put out of existence', for we still wrestle with Him even now (Eph. 6:12) but Christians will have the victory as they are on the winning side. The Christ did something no other could ever do. He took on the problem of death and solved it.

Secondly, death is defeated: Jesus Christ is the solution to death and its humiliation. Because of his words 'I am the resurrection and the life' those who trust in Jesus Christ will share in His everlasting victory (John 11:25). At the resurrection we will share in Christ's victory over death. This is what the Christian martyrs believed and why they were so willing to die.[1] Jesus Christ has, 'wiped out the handwriting of requirements that was against us' by paying our debt the law has no grounds to accuse or convict for, 'there is ... no condemnation to those who are in Christ Jesus (Rom. 8:1) and eternal life is now gifted. When the resurrection day arrives believers will be given a body like the risen Saviour; it shall be perfect, fitted for a spiritual existence and it will have the power of an endless life (1 Cor. 15:50–55). The resurrection is the triumph of Jesus Christ over 'the last enemy' death itself (1 Cor. 15:26).

Death is swallowed up in victory. O Death, where is your sting? O Hades, where is your victory?

Because of this the people of God can be confident they will rise at the last day.

Thirdly, doubt is defeated: Peter made this clear when he preached at Pentecost, 'This is what was spoken by the prophet Joel' (Acts 2:16). Pentecost was a profound and lasting fulfilment of the Father's promise for the days of Messiah. The fulfilment of Old Testament prophecies along with the outpouring of the Holy Spirit ushered in the day of grace (vv. 28–29). This removed any doubt that lingered concerning Jesus as the Christ and Saviour of the world. Here was the One predicted in the book of Psalms (by King David):

The patriarch David … being a prophet, and knowing that God had sworn with an oath to him that of the fruit of his body, according to the flesh, He would raise up the Christ to sit on his throne, he, foreseeing this, spoke concerning the resurrection of the Christ, that His soul was not left in Hades, nor did His flesh see corruption. (Acts 2:29–31)

On the Day of Pentecost (fifty days after Christ's resurrection), there and then the third person of the Trinity came in tongues of fire to burn up the dross of sin and to purify the hearts of the apostles and he graciously gave assurance of life eternal and heaven to come: 'In whom also, having believed, you were sealed with the Holy Spirit of promise' (Eph. 1:13). The Spirit's testimony is the authentication of Scripture and with it the seal of assurance. He gives assurance and hope to the heart of believers unto the end of their pilgrimage here on earth.[2]

Fourthly, difference is defeated: Paul preached the revolutionary message that we—no matter where we are from or whatever our colour or ethnicity—when found in Christ are the children of God:

For you are all sons of God through faith in Christ Jesus. For as many of you as were baptized into Christ have put on Christ. There is neither Jew nor Greek, there is neither slave nor free, there is neither male nor female; for you are all one in Christ Jesus. And if you *are* Christ's, then you are Abraham's seed, and heirs according to the promise. (Gal. 3:26–29)

It is Jesus Christ who has, by His victory over evil and sin, united all people of the earth in Himself, breaking barriers and estrangements over continents and seas. In His High Priestly prayer He asks, 'that they also may be one in Us' (John 17:21). Unity is intrinsically part of the grace of God in salvation. All who are Christ's are 'in Him' and abide in Him by faith (John 15:1–7). The unity, of which the Saviour prayed in John 17 is generated by the free grace of God and cannot be known outside union with Christ and is based upon truth, not on race, nationality or allegiance to Denominations or Assemblies. In John 17 Jesus is praying about something deeper and more miraculous than visible unity. It is a feature of Christianity, whether always properly expressed or not, between the members of congregations or those in denominations or among peoples of other colours or cultures that we 'are all one in Christ Jesus'. This is the amazing message of the New Testament which is still relevant and required today. The Bible tells us that, 'there is only *one Race*: i.e. the human race'. So there is *no* Biblical basis for racism (Gen. 9:1; Deut. 32:8; Acts 17:26). Jesus Christ is the Saviour of the world (John 3:16; Matt. 27:51; Eph. 2:14):

He hath made from one blood all nations [*ethnos*] of men for to dwell on all the face of the earth. (Acts 17:26)

Fifthly, dread defeated: from the epistle to the Romans chapter 8, we see that the glory of future resurrection life will outweigh the sufferings of our present state; this is because suffering (in whatever form) is only a temporary reality for believers and also for the creation itself. Redemption is cosmic (Rom. 8:19) and the gift of resurrection is awaited by the saints with hope (vv. 18–19); also the revitalisation of regeneration for the cosmos (vv. 19–22, cf. 2 Peter 3:10–13) while we wait for the day of resurrection:

We also who have the firstfruits of the Spirit, even we ourselves groan within ourselves, eagerly waiting for the adoption, the redemption of our body. For we were saved in this hope, but hope that is seen is not hope; for why does one still hope for what he sees? But if we hope for what we do not see, we eagerly wait for *it* with perseverance. (Rom. 8:23–25)

Christian hope prevents us being crushed by fear and dread while resurrection hope lifts up the soul and revives as we bear sufferings patiently. Our heavenly Father is committed to our (spiritual) protection and his providences are working out for our good and Christ's glory. Our pain *has* meaning and blessings (Rom. 8:22–23, 28). Jesus Christ is the firstfruits and firstborn from the dead and the hope of all who put their trust in Him. Paul also expresses the suffering of the people of God as 'light affliction':

For our light affliction, which is but for a moment, is working for us a far more exceeding *and* eternal weight of glory. (2 Cor. 4:17)

The Apostle John in his first epistle also comforts God's adopted children with the gospel hope and confirms Paul's prediction that God's people will share in Christ's victory:

There is no fear in love; but perfect love casts out fear, because fear involves torment. But he who fears has not been made perfect in love. (1 John 4:18)

By the phrase *the children of God* John is emphasising the nobility of the Christian position. So John exhorts the readers to stop and contemplate the Father's love and to marvel at his gratuitous grace, which will lead to resurrection glory at Christ's Second Coming again.

Sixthly, disbelief defeated: the resurrection three days after the burial of Jesus Christ changed the world's calendars which are dated from Jesus Christ's birth because of the resurrection. In AD 312 (Council of Nicaea) the Christian Sabbath was adopted as the first day of the week and the Christian Lord's-Day-Sabbath. Although Judaism and Islam have their own religious calendars the western world adopted a calendar dated from the coming of Jesus Christ. Jesus of Nazareth the Christ of prophecy and history.[3] Add to this the change of the Sabbath day from the last day of the week—Saturday—to the first—Sunday—and it is evident that the resurrection of Jesus Christ on the third day had a mighty impact on the world as well as the Church but not yet for Judaism which still rejects Jesus's Messianic and atoning work. With this international change the Christian Sunday Sabbath was recognised as the Lord's-Day (Rev. 1:10) and was repeated, following the Old Testament Sabbath practice, once every seven days. Thus, the world knows about the Son of God incarnate, crucified and risen from the death as its sent Saviour. From the Day of Pentecost the Church has been empowered by the Holy Spirit to declare the resurrection both as fact and gospel to the whole world. Missionaries are commissioned to 'go and tell' the good news of sins forgiven and share their resurrection hope, some are martyrs having believed in and loved Jesus Christ as their personal Saviour more than life itself.

Seventhly, further benefits of the resurrection of Christ for the Church are summarised being clearly found from John, chapter 20:

(i) Resurrection opens the way for the Holy Spirit to fill our hearts (v. 22).

By this act of God's grace the apostles (and the church) were promised to be empowered by the Holy Spirit and sent to proclaim God's plan of salvation to the Jews and Gentiles alike (cf. Acts 2:4; 10:44). Jesus had already promised the Holy Spirit to the apostles and His resurrection made this possible:

And I will pray the Father, and He will give you another Helper, that He may abide with you forever—the Spirit of truth, whom the world cannot receive. (John. 14:16–17a)

And when He has come, He will convict the world of sin, and of righteousness, and of judgment: of sin, because they do not believe in Me; of righteousness, because I go to My Father and you see Me no more; of judgment, because the ruler of this world is judged. (John. 16:5–11)

I go away to Him who sent Me, and none of you asks Me, Where are You going? ... It is to your advantage that I go away; for if I do not go away, the Helper will not come to you; but if I depart, I will send Him to you. (John 17:7)

The Holy Spirit was given to aid prayer and ministry: Jesus said to them, 'Receive the Holy Spirit' (John 20:22). He is sent to abide with believers forever. In the Old Testament the Holy Spirit came upon men at various times, but often left them. Now He would come to remain forever. The Scriptures tell us that the Spirit is given so the Church's prayers are heard. Praying is a very important aspect of the Christian life and, 'praying always ... in the Spirit' (Eph. 6:18) is the secret of powerful prayer. Prayer in the Spirit is intercession made under the influence and the instruction of the Holy Spirit: He helps our endeavours (John 14:17; Rom. 8:26). With the witness of the Spirit in our hearts, prayer is not an extra, for it, 'keeps the armour bright' and must not be neglected. The Holy Spirit calls us to true piety and a prayer life that will be powerful before God, this, every Christian can attain by 'praying always ... in the

Spirit'. W Gurnall pertinently says, 'God commands that we be not neglectful in prayer, praying always.'[4]

(ii) Resurrection secures the authority of anointed preaching, 'If you forgive the *sins* of any, they are forgiven them; if you retain the sins of any, they are retained.' (John 20:23). This refers to the preaching of the gospel of peace offered to the soul through the finished work of Christ's substitutionary sacrifice for sinners on the cross (v. 19b). Faith brings a subjective sense of reconciliation and amity to all who believe. Although the Church of Rome uses this text to authorise the power of penance and absolution by its priesthood it is far better to understand it as referring to the efficient power of gospel preaching. We reckon that the apostles did not take Jesus's words to mean that they had the power to forgive sins (see Acts 8:22). They knew that only God could forgive sins (Mark 2:7). Neither the apostles nor the church had the power to forgive specific sins or to withhold the forgiveness of any individual. Fundamentally, Jesus was speaking of the responsibility of the church to declare the gospel to the entire world, so that those who believe in Him can find the precious gift of forgiveness (Matt. 16:19). The preaching of the gospel by those filled with the Holy Spirit after Pentecost convicts the conscience of sin by the power of God's Word and it is faith (alone) in the gospel of atonement and the empty tomb that justifies the sinned before a holy God (Rom. 10:9; James 1:18, 21; 1 Peter 1:23).

(iii) Resurrection proves the deity of Jesus Christ. We have seen the Apostle Thomas was overwhelmed by this sixth appearance of the risen Saviour so much so that he could not argue against its reality. He was given the same evidence as were the other eyewitnesses a week before him; thus Thomas saw Jesus with his own eyes, he heard Him speak to him and he was challenged to physically touch 'the evidence'. For Thomas this was (more than) enough to acknowledge that Jesus, whom he loved and followed, was alive from the dead and, what is more, he could only be God incarnate, thus his words, 'My Lord and my God!'

(John 20:28). All who doubt the deity of Jesus Christ should follow Thomas in believing the evidence presented in the Gospels (and the Acts) viz. that Jesus Christ is Saviour and Lord. As the Son of God, Jesus was God and as the Saviour of humankind He is their only hope. This is why the Bible was given.

(iv) The resurrection empowered the church for mission; this is very important. A fourth fruit is seen by implication from Jesus's words to Thomas, 'because you have seen Me, you have believed. Blessed are those who have not seen and yet have believed' (v. 29). Jesus knew the gospel story (*His-story*) would be told and taken into the whole world and many believing would receive life in His name (John 20:31; 17:20). The apostles after Pentecost preached for faith in all who heard them declare the third-day resurrection of Jesus the Son of God which fulfilled Old Testament prophecy. History tells us it was blessed by the Holy Spirit and Christianity quickly spread throughout Jerusalem and Asia Minor. It must also be noted that the resurrection brought 'gifts to men' empowering the church for mission following Christ's ascension:

'*When He ascended on high, He led captivity captive, and gave gifts to men.*' (Now this, 'He *ascended*'—what does it mean but that He also first descended into the lower parts of the earth? He who descended is also the One who ascended far above all the heavens, that He might fill all things.) And He himself gave some to be apostles, some prophets, some evangelists, and some pastors and teachers, for the equipping of the saints for the work of ministry, for the edifying of the body of Christ, till we all come to the unity of the faith and of the knowledge of the Son of God, to a perfect man, to the measure of the stature of the fullness of Christ. (Eph. 4:8–12)

Conclusion

At the end of chapter 20, John, under the guidance of the Holy Spirit, reveals why the four Gospels were written:

These are written that you may believe that Jesus is the Christ, the Son of God, and that believing you may have life in His name. (v. 31)

By faith alone through Christ alone and by the grace of God alone, we are saved to the glory of God alone. A person is either a child of God or a child of the devil (1 John 3:10). The need to communicate the saving message in the Bible is so important that God has undertaken to protect its integrity and inerrancy. Its authority rests on God himself; He is its source and originator so it has power to command and power to require submission. Christianity comes from God—revealed to man, not from his mind, imagination or heart but supernaturally through holy men who were inspired by the Holy Spirit when the holy canon was in formation (2 Pet. 1:19–21). This revelation is ultimately about God and His works. The Scriptures as they now exist are sufficient to bring men to repentance and faith and must not be added to by new revelations or traditions. They can be understood by the learned and unlearned for salvation. The Spirit of God immediately inspired the autographs so that they can be read after they are copied and translated into the vernacular for light and comfort and are meant to be the final arbitrator in all matters of religion. We understand and interpret Scripture by Scripture and that alone is the judge 'by which all controversies of religion are to be determined, and all decrees of councils, opinions of ancient writers, doctrines of men, and private spirits, are to be examined'.[5]

NOTES

1 There are four different kinds of martyrdom, namely, (i) innocence as in Abel; (ii) uprightness, as in the prophets and John the Baptist; (iii) love of the law, as in the Maccabees; (iv) confession of faith, as in the apostles. For all these various causes Christ the Lamb is said to have been 'slain from the foundations of the world' (cf. The Dialogue of Caesarius): from *Heroes of Our Faith*, Vol. 1, (McLean, VA: Isaac Publishing, 2012), p. 286.

2 cf. Calvin in his *Institutes of Religion* laid stress on this (1:viii, 1:vii:5, III:1:1).

3 Jesus was born c. BC 4–6.

Chapter 8

4 W Gurnall, *The Christian in Complete Armour*, Vol. 2 (Edinburgh: The Banner of Truth, 1995), p. 291.

5 *The Westminster Confession of Faith*, chapter 1, para 10.

The Resurrection and the Lord's-Day

If, therefore, those who were brought up in the ancient order of things have come to the possession of a new hope, no longer observing the Sabbath, but living in the observance of the Lord's-Day, on which also our life has sprung up again by Him and by His death. But every Lord's-Day do ye gather yourselves together, and break bread, and give thanksgiving after having confessed your transgressions, that your sacrifice may be pure.[1]

The change of Sabbath day from the last to the first day of the week was an important and permanent consequence of Jesus Christ's resurrection. It was authorised on Jesus Christ's own authority and upheld by the apostle's preaching and teaching. It was adopted by the post-apostolic churches in the second century and onward. There is no recorded history of this change causing a schism in the New Testament Church.[2] Not only so, but the days of the week are ordered from the day he arose from the dead—the first day of the week is Sunday. Jesus Christ's resurrection also changed the world's calendar. The date of Jesus resurrection has been historically researched to AD 30–33. His personal historical reality is also confirmed by ancient writers like Jewish Josephus (AD 37–c. 100), the Roman historian Tacitus (AD 58–c. 120), Serapion and Celsus, while in the Jewish *Talmud* there are references to Christ that confirm His historicity.

Jesus Christ's resurrection bears witness to His memory and importance. He is the Lord of the Sabbath (Mark 2:28). This means that His relationship with it is unique, authoritative and ongoing. He had been at the creation of the world when the pattern of one-day-in-seven-rest was the given pattern (Gen. 1:1; John 1:3; Col. 1:16–17).

Therefore, what is permissible and what is forbidden on that day is *His* to decide. Certainly the Sabbath was never intended to prohibit works of necessity or deeds of mercy. Christians are not obligated to keep the Jewish Sabbath. That day was given to the nation of Israel.[3] The Christian Sabbath is the Lord's-Day, the first day of the week. The principle of one day in seven was established at the creation and the New Covenant requires one still (Heb. 8; Luke 24:22). Our Lord closed His discourse in Mark 2 by reminding the Pharisees that the creation Sabbath was instituted for man's benefit, 'The Sabbath was made for man and not man for the Sabbath'—i.e. not for his bondage but blessing. It is a day of privilege when, free from secular employments, believers may worship, serve others and look after their own souls.

Dominical authority

The evidence that the first day of the week (Sunday) is the Christian day of worship is beyond question.[4] Consider:

John 20:19: The risen Saviour appeared on the first day of the week after His resurrection, thus in John 20:19 we note that the apostles came together on that Sunday evening. The Puritan John Owen remarks this first day was owned by Christ and given His title or why was it called the Lord's-Day?[5] While for John Bunyan the phrase 'after eight days' (John 20:26) confirms this day is the chosen new Sabbath established by the Holy Spirit.[6] This is because on the sixth resurrection appearance Jesus attended (in His risen person) the gathered church when it met on the first Sunday after the resurrection day and *not* before. The phrase, 'after eight days ... Jesus came ... and stood in the midst' indicates that, 'this was the start of a sanctified pattern of first day worship and it became the custom of the first church in Jerusalem after the ascension.'[7] Notice that between John 20:23 and 25 nothing is said in our sacred text (in John's narrative or for that matter, in the Synoptic Gospels) about the activities of the apostles and disciples for six days between. John Bunyan correctly asks the question why is the New Testament silent between the day of Christ's resurrection and the next Sunday (after the 'eight day'). Nothing is recorded! We suggest this is because we are to concentrate on the Holy Spirit's aim, i.e. to make it clear that the resurrection of Jesus now establishes a new worship day by divine sanction.

Acts 2:1 is another powerful seal on the change of worship day from Saturday to Sunday: the Holy Spirit also sealed this new day of worship by His presence and work at Pentecost. In Acts 2:1, the disciples are found together again on Sunday (Pentecost was on the first day of the week as Pentecost was always found on the next day after the seventh-day Sabbath).[8] Thus the Holy Spirit was given on (a) Sunday (2:4) and why not on another day: Monday, Tuesday, Thursday, etc.? The first day of the week worship was sealed by the third Person of the Trinity to reinforce divine approval for the change of worship day. We can now say that the change of Sabbath day to the Lord's-Day has the authority and seal of God.

Acts 20:7: while at Troas, the apostles and the saints came together to break bread on the first day of the week (Sunday). The context here is that of apostolic worship with the breaking of bread (the Lord's Supper) and preaching. This was a profound remembering of the Lord's death *till he comes* (1 Cor. 11:26). This was the continuation of a new practice established by the apostles after Pentecost (Acts 2:44–47) and adapted to worship in the provinces of Asia.

1 Cor. 16:1–2: from here it is clear that the gathering of the people of God *on the first day of the week* was now an organised time of worship which had apostolic approval. This then was an intentionally setting aside of seventh-day Sabbath. It was commanded by the Saviour through Paul's apostolic ministry (1 Cor. 14:37) and grants the universal adoption of this new practice for the New Testament churches. Apostolic authority for this change of day is found also in 1 Cor. 11:23, and the words *'For I have received of the Lord that which was delivered to you.'* The apostles

had the infallible guidance of the Spirit and 'what they ordained was no less of divine institution if it had been appointed by Christ in his own person'.[9]

Heb. 4:8–10 says Christ's day of rest is the Sunday for on it he ceased from His own works having conquered death by His rising again. Sunday being the day of rest for the Son of God, 'it must be the day of rest for his church also' said Bunyan.[10] In this light Bunyan also said 'he takes away the seventh day but does he leave no day for the saints to gather for worship? No. The seventh day is gone with its shadows but the divine stamp is there upon the first day if we would acknowledge it'.[11]

The third day sign

It is not just the resurrection but also the named day on which He arose that is the sign that proclaims Christ's glory and messianic mission (this roots it in both time and history). God has this pattern and gift of rest for the world today. We cannot see the Christ in His resurrected and glorified body for He is in heaven, nor were we at the resurrection event itself but the eyewitnesses have recorded it for us in the New Testament. However, the weekly Christian Sabbath, every first day of the week, points fifty-two times a year to His triumph over death and over Satan. This is a powerful witness to the mission and gospel of Jesus Christ. Without a weekly Christian Lord's-Day-Sabbath the resurrection would be so marginalised it would hardly be noticed after 2,000 years. However, God has seen to it that it is still remembered and not only by the church but also by the world through the weekly event we call the Lord's-Day or the Christian Sabbath. If the churches should stop meeting on the first day of the week the powerful witness of the Christian Lord's-Day-Sabbath would be lost. If there is no Sabbath, then the sign of the resurrection will be lost. If believers stop gathering together to worship on Sundays then this powerful testimony will be silenced.

The change of day has our Lord's authority so the apostles separated and appointed the first day of the week for holy worship. Richard Baxter said that the Christians of the apostolic age knew before the Scriptures were written that the Lord's-Day was set apart as holy. There was no need to tell them what they were already practising. The New Testament and the universal tenor and practice of the churches is the history that we must follow.[12] Bunyan sums the proofs for a change of day under the New Covenant saying that this is the first day of church worship, because (i) Christ began it on *that* day (the day of his resurrection); (ii) the Holy Ghost seconded *that* day at Pentecost (it was a Sunday when the Spirit came on the New Testament Church); (iii) the churches practised it on *that* day (as seen above); and (iv) Revelation 1:10 sanctions *that* day to the churches to the end of the world by calling it 'the Lord's-Day'.[13] There is an obvious accumulative message in the New Testament that the first day of the week is now and for all time the market day of the soul. From all the above the Apostle John's words in Revelation 1:10 are to be clearly understood as referring:

To the day of the Lord's resurrection, the first day of the week, set aside by the apostles under the direction of the Holy Spirit as a day of special worship and consecration to take the place of the seventh day Sabbath of the old dispensation.[14]

The gospel sign

The cleansing of the temple was a startling act by which the Jews discerned the messianic claim of Jesus and accordingly they sought a sign from Him. They asked, '"What sign do you show to us?" Jesus answered and said to them, "Destroy this temple, and in three days I will raise it up"' (John 2:18–22). There was a sign to come and resurrection on the third day was that sign. In this engagement with Jesus the Jews were looking for 'a sign of legitimation'.

The second temple in Jerusalem, according to the Jewish historian Josephus, was begun in the eighteenth year of Herod the Great which was *c.* 20 BC but it was not complete until AD 66; this meant that this conversation was held in the spring of AD 27.[15] Nevertheless, Jesus's words were a reference to His own future resurrection. The temple was the place where God dwelt so it was a type of Christ and was the dwelling place of the Holy Spirit. Now the new temple is the church.[16] Matthew's Gospel makes it clear that the sign the Jews were seeking would be the resurrection of Christ from the dead the sign of Jonah is the resurrection:

For as Jonah was three days and three nights in the belly of the great fish, so will the Son of Man be three days and three nights in the heart of the earth. (Matt. 12:40)

They wanted to see a miracle; they wanted him to authenticate His claim as the Prophet and reformer. This desire of the Jews was a repeated demand throughout Christ's ministry (Matt. 12:38–39; 16:1ff; Luke 11:29, 30).

Jonah was a type of Christ and the resurrection the sign for the world that Jesus Christ is the Lord of glory. The resurrection took place on Sunday, i.e. the Christian Lord's-Day, the first day of the week (John 20). The sign of Jonah was Christ's resurrection on the *third day* and on the *first day* of the week. This day is also called the *eighth day* (John 20:26) indicating, as I stated earlier, that the Jews took any part of the day as the whole day when counting up a time period in first-century Palestine. It is not just the resurrection but also the day on which He arose that is the sign that proclaims Christ's glory and messianic mission (this roots the event in both time and history).

The Church Fathers

We have noted above that the Church Fathers' acceptance of the change of Sabbath day in Ignatius' *Letter to the Church of Magnesia* and Justin Martyr's *The Didache*. Both texts were written in the second century AD. However, they are not alone in dealing with the issue. Justin Martyr (martyred *c.* AD 165) in his First Apology, declares, 'we all hold this common gathering on Sunday, since it is the first day … and Jesus Christ our Saviour on the same day rose from the dead … and on the day after Saturday, He appeared to His Apostles and disciples.'[17] James Gilfillan has recorded that 'Among the Fathers of the early Christian writers, no fewer than 31 out of 47 have adverted (referred to), with less or more brevity to the Sabbatic institution.' Gilfillan notes that in the first century two uninspired writers make reference to the change of Sabbath day; Clemens Romanus (AD 68–70) who referred to, 'the seasons of worship as by Christ instituted' and the epistle of Barnabas (AD 72) which expressly mentions the universal celebration by the church of the eighth day as a holy day, in place of the former seventh day. Tertullian (150–220), Origen (185–253), Eusebius (261–340) in his 'Ecclesiastical History', etc., they all write in support of the Sabbath change of day.[18]

God's contemporary sign

God-given signs are operative today. Men sent from God preaching faith and repentance was a sign from God in Bible times and is still so today. God expects us to listen and respond in faith to the gospel story. The resurrection was the ultimate sign for the apostles. Jesus spoke of His resurrection to the disciples during His earthly ministry but He broke the news slowly and from time to time. Peter's confession to Jesus's messianic role, however, was a turning point in the understanding of the disciple as to who Jesus was: 'You are the Christ, the Son of the living God' (Matt. 16:16). From then on Jesus spoke of His death and resurrection even more often (Matt. 16:21; 17:9, 22–23; 20:17–19). The weekly Christian Lord's-Day-Sabbath is God's sign to the world about the resurrection of Jesus Christ from the dead. Many disregard the importance of this witness because they have failed to understand the significance of first-day worship to the resurrection which speaks the gospel message universally in all nations where the church exists. It is incumbent on the churches to keep this truth alive not only as dogma but in the practice of weekly one-day-in-seven-worship that highlights the Saviour's historical third-day resurrection before a lost world. The weekly Lord's-Day is a weekly living testimony to the ascended Saviour.

Conclusion

The local churches are to meet on the first day of the week, and to ignore this public testimony will obliterate the ordained signpost to Jesus Saviour of the world. This powerful (local) witness of the Christian's testimony to the risen Saviour is vital for the success of the gospel message. If there is no Lord's-Day-Sabbath then this essential witness will be lost. If believers stop gathering together for public worship on the Lord's-Day (twice should be the norm!) then a weekly and powerful testimony ordained by God will be silenced. The Sabbath day was given to the world as a sign of atonement, reconciliation and forgiveness declaring God is love through His worshipping people.

Cultural relevance

The Lord's-Day is the ordained day of gathered local church worship. When it comes to the authority and sufficiency of the Scriptures pragmatism must not rule for the sake of cultural relevance. The desire to be culturally contemporary draws concerns of antinomianism. Sunday sports and paid-for recreations are enemies of the Lord's-Day because they keep people from the house of God and the full observance of the ordained worship. Anything that diminishes the authority, sufficiency and relevance of the Scriptures is to be challenged. The practice of a half Lord's-Day-Sabbath affects the witness of the local churches and as a result the one-day-in-seven witness of the resurrection is compromised. How can the local church be spiritually healthy when its members are not in the house of prayer and at worship but rather in front of the TV longer than they are at worship? Will the world believe if the believers are disobedient? Separation unto holiness is an effective witness. The sanctification of God's people is an issue here. Separation from the world is a clear goal for the writers of the New Testament (2 Cor. 6–7:1). If holy passion for the presence of God is lacking then the joy of the Lord is lost to the soul and their strength in the Spirit is diminished. It was Jonathan Edwards who is credited with saying, 'True religion, in great part, consists in holy affections.'[19] Where religion in the soul is true and pure says Edwards, love and joy are known. Where are holy love, joy and strength if the churches are empty on the Lord's-Day-Sabbath? Is it not true that we should be relentless in our pursuit of God's love in the soul? Only among the gathered church is this achieved.

A revival issue

Public worship one-day-in-seven is a revival issue and, as such, is very important to the health of the churches, denominations and even the nation. 'More people have been saved on the Lord's-Day than on another day of the week' (Jonathan Edwards). The reviving and empowering of the church is dependent on the rejection of worldliness and its commitment to Lord's-Day observance. The doctrine of the Lord's-Day-Sabbath is not legalism nor is it any more restrictive than any other holiness doctrine. It was understood as a delight in the Old Testament (Isa. 58:13) and also in the New. Luke's account in Acts 20:7–11 of the local church at worship on the first day of the week in Troas with Paul preaching until sunrise was anything but dull, rather the power of God was there and the preaching was long but also edifying.

Keeping the Lord's-Day holy proclaims that there is a New Covenant between God and sinners. Every time believers attend Lord's-Day worship and sanctify one day in seven to God they testify to the world that their Saviour has risen from the dead. Sunday is that one special day on which the people of God are called to gather for worship. If it were not for the Christian Sabbath (says Jonathan Edwards,) there would be little public and visible appearance of serving, worshipping and reverencing the supreme and invisible being.[20] When Christians go to church Sunday by Sunday they testify to the empty tomb proclaiming to unbelieving Jews and Gentiles alike that Jesus Christ is Lord and Messiah. Every Lord's-Day-Sabbath is a signpost to the resurrection of Jesus Christ after three days in the tomb and on the first day of the week. The creation Sabbath day was given to the world as a sign (Gen. 2:2–3; Ex. 20:8f). The Christian Lord's-Day-Sabbath (Rev. 1:10) is also a sign from God to an unbelieving world.

NOTES

1 Ignatius, *Letter to the Magnesians* 9 and *The Didache* 14.

2 James Gilfillan, *The Sabbath* (Edinburgh: A Elliot & J MacLaren, 1861), p. 17.

3 The use of the word Sabbath in the New Testament always indicates the sixth day of Jewish rest.

4 I title it 'Lord's-Day-Sabbath' because it is the day of spiritual worship and physical respite.

5 John Owen (1616–1683), *The Works of John Owen*, ed. W H Goold, Vol. 18 (Edinburgh: The Banner of Truth, 1977), p. 424.

6 When John Bunyan wrote about the Lord's-Day in 1685 he dealt with the change of day from the seventh to the first in his work, 'Questions about the Nature and Perpetuity of the Seventh-Day Sabbath', *The Works of John Bunyan* (London: Blackie and Son, 1861). He said Sunday has the badge of the Lord's glory upon it because divine grace is put into it, as it is the day of weekly commemoration of the resurrection (Matt. 28:1–10). See, Vol. 2, p. 338.

7 Ibid. p. 374.

8 The seventh Sunday after Easter, commemorates the descent of the Holy Spirit upon the apostles.

9 Owen, *Works*, Vol. 18, p. 425.

10 Bunyan, 'Questions', *Works*, Vol. 2, p. 371.

11 Ibid. p. 382.

12 Richard Baxter (1615–1691), *Practical Works*, vol. XIII (London: James Duncan, 1830), pp. 370–414.

13 Bunyan, 'Questions', *Works*, Vol. 2, p. 378.

14 Hoeksema, *Behold He Cometh*, p. 34.

15 William Hendrickson, *The Gospel of John* (London: The Banner of Truth Trust, 1969), p. 36.

16 It may have had a secondary reference to the temple for it was destroyed in AD 70, but we know that it was a reference to His future resurrection because the Holy Spirit has told us so in John 2:20–21. Herman Ridderbos has said that Jesus's body, 'is the temple that replaces the existing temple and in whom the indwelling of God among people will be truly realised … he announces a new way of worshipping God … true worshippers would worship the Father in Spirit and truth (John 4:23)'. See Herman Ridderbos, *The Gospel of John*, p. 120; cf. W Hendriksen, John, p. 125.

17 Leslie W Barnard, *St Justin Martyr the First and Second Apologies: Ancient Christian Writers*, ed. W J Bughardt (New York, N/J: Paulist Press, 1997), p. 71.

18 Gilfillan, *The Sabbath*, pp. 8–21.

19 Jonathan Edwards, *The Religious Affections, Selected Works*, Vol. 3 (London: The Banner of Truth, 1961), pp. 23–24.

20 Jonathan Edwards, 'The Perpetuity and Change of the Sabbath', *Works*, Vol. 2 (Edinburgh: Banner of Truth, 1974), p. 101.

The ascended Saviour

If we neglect our Saviour's ascension and continuing work, we risk losing sight of his unique and central place in the life of the church. (Derek Prime)

His exaltation begun at his resurrection, and received its accomplishment by his sitting at God's right hand. (Thomas Manton)[1]

The topic of the heavenly session of Christ is relevant to the Christian doctrine of the resurrection and is so important that it must not be missed. To neglect this is to miss out on understanding the Christ's messianic provision and ministry post His ascension to heaven. Our salvation is established by the facts of the Incarnation, life, death, resurrection, ascension and—not to be forgotten—the heavenly session of Jesus Christ. The ascension brought glory to Christ. By it, He exalted human nature and took it into the realms of glory previously forbidden to it. At the resurrection of the body, believers will share in the glory of Christ (but not His essential nature as God), as Thomas Manton has said, "His exultation answered his humiliation; his death was answered by his resurrection, his going into the grave by his ascending to heaven, and his lying in the grave by his sitting at God's right hand, which is a privilege proper to Christ glorified. In other words we share with him, we rise, we ascend, but we do not sit at God's right hand."[2]

All that is recorded in the book of Acts and all that the church does for the glory of God is grounded on the doctrine of the ascension of Jesus into heaven to sit at the right hand of the Father (Heb. 1:3). This historical event is recorded in Matt. 28:18–20; Mark 16:19–20; Luke 24:49 and Acts 1:9–11. The four Gospels complete the definitive recorded history of the life and work of Jesus Christ and the book of Acts is the story of the New

Testament Church beginning with the ascension of the Lord Jesus Christ into heaven forty days after His resurrection from the dead. When Jesus rose from the dead He was selective about His witnesses. These were 'witnesses chosen before God' (Acts 10:41) and not the chief priests and scribes who had challenged Him. As John Murray said, 'the chosen witnesses were able to evaluate the evidence and receive it for what it was, convincing proof'.[3] On the Mount of Olives they saw that the One who was buried was now alive:

When He had spoken these things, while they watched, He was taken up, and a cloud received Him out of their sight. And while they looked steadfastly toward heaven as He went up, behold, two men stood by them in white apparel, who also said, 'Men of Galilee, why do you stand gazing up into heaven? This *same* Jesus, who was taken up from you into heaven, will so come in like manner as you saw Him go into heaven.' (Acts 1:9–11)

All that is recorded in the book of Acts and all that the church does for the glory of God, after the crucifixion and resurrection of Jesus is dependent on the doctrine of His ascension into heaven to sit at the right hand of the Father. The ascension happened ten days before the outpouring of the Holy Spirit at Pentecost. If His ascension had not happened the *Helper* (*Paraclete*—Holy Spirit) would not have come to them. Jesus said that He must go away before the Spirit would descend on the church and give gifts to men: 'Nevertheless I tell you the truth. It is to your advantage that I go away; for if I do not go away, the Helper will not come to you; but if I depart, I will send Him to you' (John 16:7). His ascension into heaven granted the church its unique authority, equipped it for its ongoing ministry and guarantees its final victory.

Chapter 10

Old Testament Prophecy predicts Jesus Christ's ascension

Jesus Christ's resurrection was prophesied in the Psalms and speaks of the Messiah sitting at God's right hand in heaven:

The LORD (*Jehovah*) said to my Lord (*Adoni*) 'Sit at My right hand, till I make Your enemies Your footstool.' (Ps. 110:1)

Three Psalms help us here: in Psalm 110, King David is looking forward prophetically to his greater future son, the Messiah, and Jesus's use of it confirms its messianic importance (Matt. 22:46). In Psalm 24, the ascension of the Messiah into heaven was set to music in the Jewish Psalter, 'Lift up your heads, O you gates! And be lifted up, you everlasting doors! And the King of glory shall come in. Who is this King of glory? The Lord strong and mighty, the Lord mighty in battle' (Ps. 24:7–8). Again in Psalm 68, we read a prophecy about Christ's ascension into heaven, 'You have ascended on high, You have led captivity captive; You have received gifts among men, even *from* the rebellious, that the Lord [*Adoni*] God might dwell *there*' (Ps. 68:18; cf. Eph. 4:8). Thus we see that the messianic High Priestly office of Jesus Christ was recognised, recorded and foretold in the Old Testament. Having ascended into the 'heaven of heavens' (1 Kgs. 8:27) the priestly office of our Saviour is not redundant but now fully active.

Ye gates, Lift up your heads on high:
    Ye doors that last for aye,
Be lifted up, that so the King
    Of glory enter may!
But who of glory is the King?
    The mighty Lord is this,
E'en that same Lord that great in might
    And strong in battle is.
            (Scottish Psalter, 1650)

The New Testament declares Jesus Christ's ascension

This doctrine is found for the most part in the epistle of Paul to the Romans and the epistle to the Hebrews but its theme is not limited to both. In the first chapter of the epistle to the Ephesians we learn that He rose from the dead and was seated at the Father's right hand in heaven with:

Power toward us who believed ... which He worked in Christ when He raised Him from the dead and seated *Him* at His right hand in the heavenly *places*, far above all principality and power and might and dominion, and every name that is named, not only in this age but also in that which is to come. (Eph. 1:19b–21)

In this prayer Paul asks for growth in grace which is the produce of the resurrection and also the blessing of the heavenly ministry of the ascended Christ. He notes Christ's power when seated at the right hand of God the Father and the continuation of His people's sanctification unto consummation in glory. Jesus Christ, the Theanthropos (God-man), with ascended power is 'far above' all and sits with universal dominion now and forever to fulfil His Mediatorial work on the church's behalf (Matt. 28:18; Phil. 2:9–11). This dominion is over the angels (Eph. 3:10, 6:12; cf. Rom. 8:38; Col. 1:16) and because 'all *things* [are] under His feet' he is the ruler of the universe as well as the church:

And gave Him *to be* head over all *things* to the church, which is His body, the fullness of Him who fills all in all. (Eph. 1:22–23)

This exaltation and dominion includes the devils and kings, and so-called future 'prophets'. In the book of Revelation we read, 'Jesus Christ, the faithful witness, the firstborn from the dead, and the ruler over the kings of the earth' (Rev. 1:5).

Chapter 10

Romans

The practice of personal prayer and spiritual comfort for all of God's people is predicated not only on Christ's vicarious work of atonement but also on His resurrection and ascension. In the epistle to the Romans, (8:34), Paul asks:

Who *is* he who condemns? *It is* Christ who died, and furthermore is also raised, who is even at the right hand of God, who *also* makes intercession *for us*. (Rom. 8:34)

In this verse the risen Jesus Christ's saving work is summarised as it stresses the fact that His works of righteousness and power were all done '*for us*'. Jesus Christ lived for us keeping the law on our behalf and died in our place to reconcile us to a holy God. He acted always on behalf of God's people as their Mediator and Representative. Four glorious events are highlighted in verse 34: His death, resurrection, ascension and His heavenly session at God's right hand. These combine to declare that 'there is no other name under heaven given among men by which we must be saved' (Acts 4:12). They also conclude, as Paul's emphasis in the opening verse of Romans chapter 8 make clear, 'There is now no condemnation to those who are in Christ Jesus'. Christ's saving work was for the personal and eternal salvation of those who would believe in Him. Because of Christ Jesus's saving work as Mediator and Representative, sin is defeated once for all time through the cross and all who approach God in faith through Jesus Christ are declared righteous. Thus it is good to remember that He 'is even at the right hand of God, who *also* makes intercession for us'.

Hebrews

The author of the epistle to the Hebrews, as part of his introduction to the person and work of Jesus Christ, takes us quickly to the theme of ascension by quoting from Psalm 110:

But to which of the angels has He ever said: 'Sit at My right hand, till I make Your enemies Your footstool'? (Heb. 1:13)

This opening gambit leads the way to a clear doctrine of the exaltation and messianic heavenly session of Jesus Christ. The author thought that this topic was so important that he devoted about four chapters to the topic:

Seeing then that we have a great High Priest who has passed through the heavens, let us therefore come boldly to the throne of grace, that we may obtain mercy and find grace to help in time of need. (Heb. 4:14, 16)

From this epistle we note:

(I) CHRIST'S ASCENSION GLORY IS UNIQUE

Our Saviour seated in the heaven of heavens declares His kingly dignity and glory. He is at the right hand of the throne of God, 'Higher expression cannot be used to lead us into a holy adoration of the tremendous invisible glory that is intended.'[4] This eternal and glorious Saviour is the giver and the Sustainer of our salvation:

Looking unto Jesus, the author and finisher of our faith, who for the joy that was set before Him endured the cross, despising the shame, *and has sat down at the right hand of the throne of* God! (Heb. 12:2)[5]

This text flags up his unique divinity and majesty. Thus His sovereignty, glory, power and authority are shown and are eternally active, 'Now *this is* the main point of the things we are saying: We have such a High Priest, who is seated at the right hand of the throne of the Majesty in the heavens' (Heb. 8:1). This was the very glory the psalmist foretold (Ps. 68:18) and Paul speaks of in his epistle to the Ephesians:

'Therefore He says: "When He ascended on high, He led captivity captive, and gave gifts to men"' (4:8b–10). It was this ascended and seated Theanthropos that John saw in his vision while on the island of Patmos (Rev. 1:13–17). Jesus ascended to the majesty on high to be crowned with glory and honour (John 17:5) and by it He exalted human nature and took it into the realms of glory previously forbidden to it.[6] At the resurrection, the justified will share in the glory of Christ (but not His essential nature as God), 'being united with his divine person and given immortality, power, knowledge and grace and made free from infirmities'.[7] In heaven He is attended by ten thousand times ten thousand angelic spirits who worship Him saying with a loud voice, 'Worthy is the Lamb who was slain to receive power and riches and wisdom, and strength and honour and glory and blessing!', and they are joined by every creature which is in heaven, on the earth, under the earth and the twenty-four elders who all give honour and worship to God and the Lamb (Rev. 5:11–13). The ascension means the risen Saviour is now our Heavenly Advocate (1 John 2:1) and in heaven he continues His Highly Priestly office on behalf of those redeemed by His atoning blood.

As King

The Ascended Saviour, seated in heaven and reigning over His Church as King. He is the head of the Church both triumphant and militant.[8] Our Redeemer Saviour reigns over all powers spiritual as well as temporal. This authority and dignity is Christ's as Creator from everlasting as God the Son (John 17:5). His authority is over nature, the world and all creation visible and invisible and in His session He rules a kingdom of heavenly power: 'And He put all *things* under His feet, and gave Him *to be* head over all *things* to the church, which is His body, the fullness of Him who fills all in all' (Eph. 1:22–23). As King Regent He reigns until all enemies are under His feet at the end of the age:

For He must reign till He has put all enemies under His feet. The last enemy that will be destroyed is death. For '*He has put all things under His feet.*' Now when all things are made subject to Him, then the Son Himself will also be subject to Him who put all things under Him, that God may be all in all. (1 Cor. 15:25–28)

His authority was this very thing the Pharisees challenged: 'Now when He came into the temple, the chief priests and the elders of the people confronted Him as He was teaching, and said, "By what authority are You doing these things? And who gave You this authority?"' (Matt. 21:23). As Victor over death and hell He told His disciples:

'All authority has been given to Me in heaven and on earth', adding, 'Go therefore and make disciples of all the nations, baptizing them in the name of the Father and of the Son and of the Holy Spirit, teaching them to observe all things that I have commanded you; and lo, I am with you always, *even* to the end of the age. Amen.' (Matt. 28:18–20)

While in heaven his reign is spiritual: he said, 'The Kingdom of God is within you' (Lk. 17:21; Matt. 10:27; Rom. 14:17). Believers are to be salt and light in a fallen world doing good works and living holy lives while ruled by the ascended and reigning King of the Church. After the Saviour (the Theanthropos—the God-man) has subdued all His enemies and the work of redemption is done, 'He will no longer reign over the universe as Mediator, but only as God, while His headship over His people is to continue forever' (1 Cor. 15:24).[9]

As Shepherd

As Mediator, Jesus is seated in heaven watching His sheep as the Good Shepherd. The task of saving sinners rests on the shoulders of Jesus the Good Shepherd. He came to save His people from their sins. This was *His* calling and *His* commission alone, 'I am the good shepherd. The good shepherd gives His life for the sheep' (John 10:11). Now seated in heaven as King and as their Shepherd:

He who sits on the throne will dwell among them. They shall neither hunger anymore nor thirst anymore; the sun shall not strike them, nor any heat; for the Lamb who is in the midst of the throne will shepherd them and lead them to living fountains of waters. And God will wipe away every tear from their eyes. (Rev. 7:15–17)

His death and intercessions for *His* redeemed sheep are proof of *His* love and *His* care seen also in this watchful undertaking seated at the right hand of God in heaven.

As Redeemer

Although Jesus Christ is no longer on earth and He lives in heaven; this has great implication for the Church's salvation. The ascension is the necessary sequel to the resurrection.

Notice:

- It was an historical event visibly witnessed by the apostles and it took place forty days after His resurrection. 'Ascension Day' is a day in the Christian calendar forever fixed in history (Acts 1:9–11). Charles Hodge says, Jesus Christ, 'clothed in our nature, having a true body and soul', passed through the heavens into the dwelling place of God (Heb. 4:14).
- Christ's ascension recognised that the work of Jesus Christ is complete and acceptable to God the Father. Because of this Christ is deserving of exaltation. It was Christ's Coronation Day: 'Lift up your heads, O you gates! And be lifted up, you everlasting doors! And the King of glory shall come in' (Ps. 24:7). He has entered heaven to reign as its Prince, being crowned with glory and honour (Heb. 2:9).
- Jesus Christ did not rise from the dead to start a new life on earth

all over again; no, He rose that He might ascend to glory into the true tabernacle, the most holy place, heaven itself, and there to sit at God's right hand (Heb. 1:3; 8:2; 9:12, 24).

- The enthroned Christ is the head of the church for all ages: 'He raised Him from the dead and seated *Him* at His right hand in the heavenly *places*, far above all principality and power and might and dominion, and every name that is named, not only in this age but also in that which is to come. And He put all *things* under His feet, and gave Him *to be* head over all *things* to the church' (Eph. 1:20–22).

- His human nature is glorified not deified. He has crowned human nature with glory and lifted it above that of the angels and archangels. As another said, 'God dignified our nature for he has given us grace and some day glory too. He sits there and it will not be long before all the redeemed sit there too' (Rev. 3:21; 5:6).[10] The ascension of Jesus opened the door through which the ransomed and resurrected dead can enter heaven. (Rev. 7:14).

Conclusion

Let us remember that heaven is the place when Christ dwells. The Bible believes in a place called heaven.

- God is in heaven
- Jesus came from heaven
- Jesus went back to heaven
- Angels ascend and descend from heaven
- The Holy Spirit was sent from heaven

When one thinks about heaven then one needs to think about the distinction that the Bible makes between (1) disembodied spirits and (2) resurrected bodies. It helps to keep these two separate as this will keep us from confusing the information that is available to us on the topic of heaven. The former (1) is after death and the latter follows the resurrection of the body. One is existence in a celestial body and the other in the resurrected body. But it is valid to call both heaven. The first is the heaven of 'just men made perfect' (Heb. 12:23) the second the heaven of the 'new heavens and the new earth' (Rev. 21:1).

Jesus Christ's ascension is good news for sinners and saints alike. Because He lives forever, 'He is also able to save to the uttermost those who come to God through Him' (Heb. 7:25). God calls us by His Spirit to repent and believe the gospel. Personal prayer is an act of faith which calls out from the soul to the Son of God who has ascended and is seated on high at God's right hand:

Seeing then that we have a great High Priest who has passed through the heavens, Jesus the Son of God, let us hold fast *our* confession … Let us therefore come boldly to the throne of grace, that we may obtain mercy and find grace to help in time of need. (Heb. 4:14, 16)

This means that those saved by grace are to live their lives, 'Looking unto Jesus, the author and finisher of *our* faith, who for the joy that was set before Him endured the cross, despising the shame, and has sat down at the right hand of the throne of God' (Heb. 12:2). In the light of this, God's people can sing with new understanding the chorus:

Because He lives I can face tomorrow;
Because He lives all fear is gone;
Because I know He holds the future,
And life is worth the living
Just because He lives.'
(W J Gaither)

NOTES

1 Thomas Manton, *An Exposition of John 17* (Wilmington, DE: Sovereign Grace, 1972), p. 91.
2 Ibid.

3 John Murray, *Collected Writings*, Vol. 1 (Edinburgh: Banner of Truth Trust, 1982), p. 43.

4 Owen, Vol. 22, p. 10.

5 Emphasis mine.

6 In John 17:5 Jesus says, 'O Father, glorify Me together with Yourself, with the glory which I had with You before the world was.'

7 Manton, *John 17*, p. 91.

8 These terms are valid distinctions when speaking about the church in heaven and on earth.

9 Hodge, *The First Epistle to the Corinthians*, p. 330.

10 Unknown author.

Heavenly intercession

If we are Christians we shall find it essential to our comfort in religion to have clear views of Christ's priestly office and intercession. Christ lives, and therefore our faith shall not fail. He is at the right hand of God. (J C Ryle)[1]

When we presume to pray to God, we will be rejected unless Jesus Christ is there on our behalf. And because he is there he is our Intercessor, who causes our prayers to reach God and who allows us to have them answered. Now since our Lord Jesus Christ has entered heaven and since he carries us there … [and] he bears us on his heart, we should not have any doubts when we pray to God. (John Calvin)[2]

Christ's session, now that He is seated in heavenly places, is eternal. There, Jesus's prayer ministry for His people is unique; His eternal priesthood will never be passed on to others nor will there be an interruption or termination to its effectiveness. It cannot be passed on because it is after the 'order of Melchizedek' the 'King of Salem, priest of the Most High God' and now having risen from the dead He possesses the 'power of an endless life' (Heb. 7:1a). Others have tried to take this role for themselves; however, Christ Jesus is the only (High) Priest of the Church:

The Lord has sworn and will not relent, 'You are a priest forever according to the order of Melchizedek,' by so much more Jesus has become a surety [guarantee] of a better covenant. (Heb. 7:21–22)

While in session the Saviour's people are continually upon His *mind*; and they are continually near His *heart*. Even as Israel's high priest bore the names of the twelve tribes upon his breastplate, so He is always thinking of His blood-bought children. The eyes of the Lord never sleep and are perpetually watching over their welfare (Ps. 121). Is it not true that *we* always pray for those whom *we* love? Loving His Bride the Church, Jesus Christ prays for it unceasingly. Even personal sin cannot keep us from God's covenant blessings when saved. This Charles Spurgeon rejoices to acquaint us with: 'all the foolishness and ignorance which David had just been confessing to God [Ps. 73:22], not one atom the less was it true and certain that David was saved and accepted, and that the blessing of being constantly in God's presence was undoubtedly his.'[3] When seated 'in Christ' in heavenly places the Christian is reckoned righteous in God's sight. This was the great gospel truth that Luther came to understand when he studied Paul's epistle to the Romans, 'the righteousness of God is revealed from faith to faith; as it is written, "The just shall live by faith"' (Rom. 8:17).

What does Jesus pray for us?

In heaven our Saviour's love is seen in His intercessions for us. In session Christ Jesus lives with the Father and the angels and his high priestly ministry on behalf of his people continues and at the Father's side where he is perpetually applying the shed blood of sacrifice, 'in order to obtain for them the fruits of that oblation'.[4] Spurgeon also comments on this, 'In all the incense which our Great High Priest now puts into the golden censer, there is not a single grain for himself. As high priest the sprinkled blood first offered on earth is now offered in heaven.'[5] While John Brown in his *Discourses and Sayings of Our Lord*, tell us that Jesus prays, 'the Father [to] send forth the Holy Spirit to produce faith that they may be justified, and continue to strengthen their faith, that they may be sanctified'.[6] Christ presents His death to God in continual intercession for His people. This heavenly ministry allows Him to 'save to the uttermost those who come to God through Him since He always lives to make intercession for us' (Heb. 7:25), and because He appears before God, as Calvin notes, 'in our name, that our prayers are cleansed by the sprinkling of his blood. Our prayers must be cleaned by the sprinkling of blood to be free from uncleanness.'[7]

It is also clear that our loving Saviour prays for our perseverance in the faith until heaven is reached. Jesus's words to the Apostle Peter in Luke 22:31–32 make clear His (covenant) commitment to Peter, and by extension to all the blood-bought people of God, that He will pray for each one in days of temptation and trouble. The Good Shepherd King will care for all His sheep. He will ensure that their faith does not fail and *also* that their service to God will continue through the ups and downs of their pilgrimage and ministries:

> And the Lord said, 'Simon, Simon! Indeed, Satan has asked for you, that he may sift *you* as wheat. But I have prayed for you, that your faith should not fail; and when you have returned to *Me*, strengthen your brethren.' (Luke 22:31)

The people of God can be assured of help and blessing to come. This is because, as the apostle puts it, they 'have an Advocate with the Father, Jesus Christ the righteous' (1 John 2:1). Assurance of protection for God's people is grounded on Jesus Christ's ascension to heaven following the resurrection and this is made unequivocally clear in the Gospels. J C Ryle said, 'Peter had a mighty Friend at the right hand of God because, "There is a watchful Advocate, who is daily pleading for him, seeing all his daily necessities, and obtaining daily supplies of mercy and grace for his soul."'[8] The eternal protection of the Apostle Peter and all the people of God rests on Christ Jesus's perpetual intercession for them and not on themselves or other mediation. His eternal ministry for them at God's right hand can never be hijacked. When God's people sin, Jesus represents them as their 'Advocate with the Father':

> My little children, these things I write to you, so that you may not sin. And if anyone sins, we have an Advocate with the Father, Jesus Christ the righteous. (1 John 2:1)

Psalm 121

We find an illustration in the Old Testament which gives a clear picture of the Lord's work while in His session. The psalmist speaks with personal faith, 'My help *comes* from the Lord, who made heaven and earth (v. 2). In this Psalm we are guaranteed that God will keep His children from slipping or falling; there is the guarantee of deliverance 'from all evil' (v. 7) and there is a promise of a guardian who, 'shall neither slumber nor sleep' (v. 4). There is hope from promises (great and precious) that the beloved sheep of the Shepherd King shall be sheltered from every evil power day and night, 'The sun shall not strike you by day, nor the moon by night' (v. 6). Jesus's trusting sheep can know that their Messiah is working all things together for good to those who love Him, who are called according to His purpose (Rom. 8:28). Thus we see that Psalm 121 is a prophetic word about Jesus Christ's heavenly session. Here is a guarantee of our Saviour's personal and deep interest in all saints individually. He 'shall preserve your soul' and He 'shall preserve your going out and your coming in from this time forth and even forevermore' (Ps. 121:7–8). From this Psalm we learn the Saviour's beloved people are close to His heart and always before His eyes watching over their welfare, 'Behold, He who keeps Israel shall neither slumber nor sleep' (v. 4).

Praying in Jesus's name only

Because the blood of the incarnate crucified Son of God was once and for always uniquely a single act of propitiatory sacrifice which never needs to be repeated, personal confession of sin is to be made to Jesus Christ alone as He is the now ascended and seated High Priest of the Church (Matt. 6:5–8). All earthly priests are obsolete as no one—no pope, or vicar, or canonised 'saint'—can replace Jesus Christ of Nazareth crucified and risen again on the third day ascended to heaven. In prayer the people of God come, 'to Jesus the Mediator of the new covenant, and

to the blood of sprinkling that speaks better things than *that of* Abel'
(Heb. 12:24). Since our heavenly High Priest, Christ Jesus, encourages
His people to come to *Him* in prayer they can to look to Him for grace in
time of need; all other priests and mediators are redundant:

Therefore, brethren, having boldness to enter the Holiest by the blood of Jesus, by a
new and living way which He consecrated for us, through the veil, that is, His flesh,
and *having* a High Priest over the house of God, let us draw near with a true heart in
full assurance of faith, having our hearts sprinkled from an evil conscience and our
bodies washed with pure water. (Heb. 10: 19–22)

He prays there 'for us' as 'A Minister of the sanctuary and of the true
tabernacle which the Lord erected, and not man' (Heb. 8:2). We are
reminded by these words of Israel's ancient high priest who once a year
on the Day of Atonement (Yom Kippur), entered the holy-of-holies in the
tabernacle with the blood of sacrifice to reconcile the people to God.
Christ Jesus the Church's true High Priest—of whom the Old Testament
priesthood was a shadow —is now seated in heaven and lives to apply all
the benefits of His atonement to all the redeemed:

He, because He continues forever, has an unchangeable priesthood. Therefore He is
also able to save to the uttermost those who come to God through Him, since He
always lives to make intercession for them. (Heb. 7:23–25)

Salvation grace is in Christ alone
We note also from the epistle of Paul to the Romans that Christ's
resurrection and ascension is not the end of the salvation story because
our Saviour is in heaven and 'makes intercession for us' (Rom. 8:34). This
verse speaks of the continuing process by which God's people are freed
from the power of sin eventually to be completed at their glorification. In
His role as intercessor, Christ Jesus is 'able to keep you from stumbling,

(falling) and to present *you* faultless before the presence of His glory with exceeding joy' (Jude 24). His work is unique: He prays for us and in heaven He is our sole and only intercessor, and because Christ Jesus has an unchangeable priesthood, 'He is able to save to the uttermost' (i.e. completely, totally and fully) all of God's people because He not only died for them but is alive to make intercession for them. This is very precious and brings assurance and peace to the soul.

> The soul that on Jesus hath leaned for repose,
>> He'll never, no never desert to his foes.
> That soul, though all hell should endeavour to shake,
>> He'll never, no never, no never forsake!
>> (Richard Keen)

There is no danger of any believer being lost because Jesus has come, died, risen and pleads 'for us'. God's people have eternal safety and protection dwelling in mystical union by faith 'in Christ'. His blood atones for sins and His works avail for us. Now since His resurrection it can be said (by us), 'be gone works of self-righteousness, penances and alms of all are obsolete now that salvation is ours through faith alone, in Christ alone' (cf., Eph. 2:8–9).

Christ's unique high priestly office

Prayers for and to the dead are therefore not warranted because they make Christ out as insufficient and unsuccessful in His intercessions for those for whom He died. Prayers to the dead dishonour Him and reject His mediatorial and High Priestly office. They also empty the cross of its efficacy and transform departed souls into gods (*deus*). Support for the Roman Catholic doctrine of supererogation does not stand up to scriptural examination.[9] Calvin spoke against this error: 'We should be certain that our prayers will always be acceptable to God, for it is through Jesus Christ that we speak. If this had been well understood there would never have been so many superstitions in popery. Why do they have so many patron saints? Why do they turn to the Virgin Mary? Because they have never understood why Jesus Christ ascended to heaven. They would have realised that Jesus Christ was in heaven for our sakes, and that we can have access to God without the need of patron saint and advocates.'[10] The dead do not (and cannot) pray for the living because there is one Mediator between God and humankind, viz. the risen and ascended Jesus Christ (Heb. 8:6; 9:16; 12:24). Redeemed and justified sinners who are adopted into the kingdom of Jesus Christ are glorified by the Son so that the whole Church, both triumphant and militant, will see Him and praise Him by means of a new power and vitality in their ransomed and redeemed bodies, which will be made like His own resurrection body. When God's people sin, Jesus represents them in heaven as the, 'Advocate with the Father': 'My little children, these things I write to you, so that you may not sin. And if anyone sins, we have an Advocate with the Father, Jesus Christ the righteous' (1 John 2:1). It is worthy of note that John does not say *with God*, but rather *with the Father*. This reminds us of the blessed truth that though sin in a believer's life breaks fellowship, it does not break that new relationship wonderfully purchased by the blood of the cross. When Satan brings some accusation against a believer, the Lord Jesus points to His finished work on Calvary. The Lord Jesus is not only our Advocate but He is also 'the propitiation for our sins' (1 John 4:10). This means that by dying for us He not only freed us from the guilt of our sins but He removed every barrier to fellowship which sin had destroyed. The justified cannot be lost. Jesus Christ will make sure of this:

Begone, unbelief, My Saviour is near,
    And for my relief will surely appear;
By prayer let me wrestle and He will perform;
    With Christ in the vessel I smile at the storm.
                (John Newton)

Eternal victory

Christ's work of vicarious redemption brings salvation to all who believe and are justified by faith only. It is also true that Christ Jesus waits for the day of the consummation of all things because He is seated in heaven as the Lord, 'both of the dead and the living' (Rom. 14:9). In Hebrews we read:

> But this Man, after He had offered one sacrifice for sins forever, sat down at the right hand of God, from that time waiting till His enemies are made His footstool. (Heb. 10:12–13)

Why does He wait? What is stopping Him coming a second time now? Four reasons are given. Firstly, He waits until all His (elect) sheep are born and gathered in from every tribe and nation. He does not wish that any should perish but that all should come to repentance (Matt. 28:19–20; 2 Peter 3: 9ff). So He waits until they are reached with the gospel message through evangelism and are sanctified by God's Word (John 17:15–18, 20). Secondly, the seated Christ is waiting, in heaven, for the last day and the decreed moment of His Second Coming. On that day He will subdue His enemies fulfilling completely the prophecy of King David, 'The LORD (*Jehovah*) said to my Lord (*Adonai*) "Sit at My right hand, till I make Your enemies Your footstool"' (Ps. 110:1).[11] The enemies of God and His church will be utterly defeated at Christ's return; 'His session is to last until the total subjection of His enemies, that is to say, this special and extraordinary power of the Messiah is then to terminate (1 Cor. 15:24–28)'.[12] Thirdly, He is there to give repentance to Israel: 'The God of our fathers raised up Jesus whom you murdered by hanging on a tree. Him God has exalted to His right hand *to be* Prince and Saviour, to give repentance to Israel and forgiveness of sins' (Acts 5:30–31, cf. Rom. 11). Fourthly, He waits for the Father to give Him the command to come a second time to earth with power and great glory (Matt. 24:30–31, 36). This 'date' the Father has reserved to himself (Mark 13:32).

Conclusion

The One who is the Keeper of Israel and coming Redeemer has promised in Psalm 121 and under the New Covenant to take care of His people and He has done so under a whole life guarantee:

The Lord shall preserve you from all evil; He shall preserve your soul. The Lord shall preserve your going out and your coming in from this time forth, and even forevermore. (Ps. 121:7–8)

He is also able to save to the uttermost those who come to God through Him, since He always lives to make intercession for them. (Heb. 7:25)

At least seven things can be noted, because Jesus Christ our Saviour ascended and sits in session:
- He keeps His sheep from falling in times of testing. Even personal sin cannot keep us from God's covenant blessings when washed in the atoning blood of the Lamb. John Calvin comments: 'It is for our sake that He ascended and is now in heaven, there is nothing in this world we have to fear.'[13]
- He strengthens the church's witness when conflicts increase. The believer can in the spirit of true submission pray, 'Send me what thou wilt, my God, so long as it comes from thee; there never came an ill portion from thy table to any of thy children.'[14]
- He hears the supplications of His people when in times of need: 'For the eyes of the Lord are on the righteous, and His ears are open to their prayers' (1 Pet. 3:12).
- He forgives their sins and rebellions and grants new (subjective)

peace (1 John 2:1–2) granting His Spirit who is the Comforter and Helper of the Church (John 14:16–18).

- He grants new obedience in the promised strength of spiritual renewal (Luke 22:32).
- He sustains hope in the soul of the glory to come and sustains the hope of rewards of faithfulness (Heb. 10:35).
- He has a place reserved for them at His side in heaven and will return for them at a time of the Father's appointing (John 14:1–2; Matt. 24:44; 25:13).

As the promised Guardian who, 'shall neither slumber nor sleep' the coming Shepherd guarantees peace and protection to all who believe and look for His coming (again). This protection is from the world, the flesh and the devil and comes via the (covenant) promises of the Scriptures and from the Lord who loved the church and gave Himself for it. The Christ who is personally involved in the life and work of His blood-bought bride is committed to her security.

Arise, my soul, arise,

Shake off thy guilty fears,

The bleeding Sacrifice

In my behalf appears;

Before the throne my Saviour stands:

My name is written on His hands.

The Father hears Him pray,

His dear anointed one;

He cannot turn away

The presence of His Son:

His Spirit answers to the blood,

And tells me I am born of God.

(Charles Wesley)

Chapter 11

NOTES

1   J C Ryle, *Expository Thoughts on the Gospels: St Luke*, Vol. 2 (London: James Clark & Co. Ltd, 1969), p. 412.

2   John Calvin, *Crucified and Risen*, trans. Robert White (Edinburgh: The Banner of Truth Trust, 2020), p. 162.

3   C H Spurgeon, *Morning & Evening*, July 29.

4   Robert Haldane, *Romans* (London: Banner of Truth, 1966), p. 416.

5   C H Spurgeon, *Morning & Evening*, 6 February.

6   John Brown, *Discourses and Sayings of Our Lord*, Vol. 3, p. 28.

7   John Calvin, *Calvin's Institutes* (Grand Rapids, MI: Associated Publishers and Authors Inc. No date), 3:20:18.

8   Ryle, *Expository Thoughts on the Gospels: St Luke*, Vol. 2, p. 411.

9   Works of supererogation: 'works which, not absolutely required of each individual for salvation, may be done for the sake of greater perfection, affording the [Roman Catholic] church a store of surplus merit, to eke out the deficient merit of others.' See, Chambers Harrap Publishers Ltd: *The Chambers Dictionary*, 2003; *The Chambers Thesaurus*, 2004.

10 Calvin, *Crucified and Risen: Sermons on Matthew 26–28* (Edinburgh, The Banner of Truth Trust, 2020), pp. 162–163.

11 This verse reveals the personal relationship David had with *Adonai* (his Lord). No psalm is more quoted in the New Testament than Ps. 110. Alexander says, 'The repeated, explicit and emphatic application of this Psalm in the New Testament, to Jesus Christ, is so far from being arbitrary or at variance with the obvious import of the psalm itself, that any other application is ridiculous.' See, J A Alexander, *The Psalms* (Welwyn: Evangelical Press, 1975), p. 457.

12 Lenski, *1 and 2 Corinthians*, pp. 671ff

13 Ibid, Calvin, *Crucified and Risen*, p.164.

14 Spurgeon, *Morning & Evening*, 5 August.

Resurrection challenge (1 Cor. 15:21–34)

Everything we know about St. Paul is consistent with the assumption that He believed the tomb of Christ to have been vacant on the morning of Easter Sunday. Nothing that we know about Him supports the suggestion that He knew it had never been disturbed. (Frank Morison)[1]

Paul's first epistle to the Corinthians is very important in constructing the Christian doctrine of the resurrection. When Paul discourses on this topic He argues for a doctrine of bodily resurrection of Jesus Christ and of those believers who will share His glory. This important chapter written from Ephesus in the spring of AD 54 or 55 at the beginning of His third missionary journey refutes the notion that this subject matter is secondary and should not divide Christendom. In the letter we are told that the story of Christ's resurrection *is* the gospel: 'Moreover, brethren, I declare to you the gospel which I preached to you, which also you received and in which you stand, by which also you are saved' (vv. 1–2). Thus Paul makes it clear that to deny the bodily resurrection of Jesus Christ is to deny the gospel (the good news). Whatever the false prophets replace it with might have sounded logical or rational or philosophically sensible or whatever, but it will *not* be the gospel no matter how eloquently conveyed (cf. Gal. 1:6–7). However, Paul in the Spirit preached the message of the gospel to the Corinthian church during his second missionary journey in AD 49–52 and he shows the importance of this doctrine in his subsequent correspondence to them.[2]

Chapter 12

Paul's theology

Paul was sure that the Old Testament prophecy foretold the resurrection of Jesus the Messiah and he spoke convincingly of its reality as well as the theology. Prior to his conversion he persecuted those who believed in the physical resurrection of Christ while after his conversion and his self-exile in Arabia (modern Iraq) his defence of it was extraordinary and can only be accounted for by his conviction after having actually met the risen Jesus Christ on the Damascus road. Paul's discussions with eyewitnesses (Peter and James) in Jerusalem no doubt cleared up any historical facts he had doubted and his personal three years of Old Testament studies during his time in Arabia combined together to settle any questions he might have had about the reality, theology and necessity of the resurrection of the incarnate Son of God. Morison says, 'Saul of Tarsus must have been abundantly informed concerning the real facts, not only from the official side [Sadducees] as regards the supposed abduction of the body, but through his disputations in the Synagogue with the Christian interpretation also'[3]:

I went to Arabia, and returned again to Damascus. Then after three years I went up to Jerusalem to see Peter, and remained with him fifteen days. But I saw none of the other apostles except James, the Lord's brother. (Gal. 1:17b–19)

Paul did not rely only on the subjective experience which led to his conversion but also asked what does the Scriptures say and what are the facts about the resurrection event? As a result he confirmed that resurrection hope was both a prophetic and theological expectation in Israel and both of which met together in the person of Jesus of Nazareth. Thereafter he was a willing martyr and he became the scholar and evangelist of the first century Church whom God raised up to record the facts and the gospel par excellence.[4] Having clarified Old Testament prophecy and that the New Testament witnesses confirmed the historic reality of the third day resurrection, Paul lays out the validity of the doctrine of the resurrection in 1 Corinthians 15, using these two (Old Testament prophecy and contemporary history) great allies to declare the miracle of Christ's resurrection.

Believing in the resurrection miracle, in Acts Paul preached the resurrection of the body before Governor Felix with a statement grounded in Daniel 12:2:

I have hope in God, which they themselves also accept, that there will be a resurrection of *the* dead, both of *the* just and *the* unjust. (Acts 24:15)

The resurrection is the seal and headstone of the great work of redemption. It is also the crowning proof that Jesus Christ delivers all those justified from judgement and hell fire. Many may reject it or deny it, and speak in philosophical terms against it but no reader of the New Testament can deny that it is there in the canon and text and that the New Testament believes in it and proclaims it as true. The physical resurrection on the third day on the first day of the week is the faith of the Christian Church:

I believe in Jesus Christ, God's only Son, our Lord, who was conceived by the Holy Spirit, born of the Virgin Mary, suffered under Pontius Pilate, was crucified, died, and was buried; He descended to the dead. On the third day He rose again; He ascended into heaven, He is seated at the right hand of the Father. (The Apostles' Creed)[5]

We believe in one Lord, Jesus Christ, the only Son of God … For our sake He was crucified under Pontius Pilate; He suffered death and was buried. On the third day He rose again … We look for the resurrection of the dead. (Nicene Creed, AD 325)[6]

THE ASSURANCE OF LIFE TO COME

That Jesus is the Vanquisher of death, re-entered life and is now reigning in heaven is expressed in the phrase 'the firstfruits'. In due season we shall rise to be like Him:

But now Christ is risen from the dead, *and* has become the firstfruits of those who have fallen asleep. For since by man *came* death, by Man also *came* the resurrection of the dead. (vv. 20–21)

Our Saviour is by resurrection the first in *time*, therefore we shall share in the promised resurrection; and first in *kind*, therefore we will be same in spiritual kind; and first in *pledge*, therefore resurrection is the promise yet to come. This hope rests in the heart of the believer, 'we also who have the firstfruits of the Spirit, even we ourselves groan within ourselves, eagerly waiting for the adoption, the redemption of our body' (Rom. 8:23). So we are assured that in Christ we will be raised from the dead too.

THE ASPECTS OF LIFE TO COME

It was Adam who messed things up in Eden and it is 'the last Adam' (v. 45) who came to fix it: 'man [was] the death medium' says Lenski, 'man [was] also the resurrection medium.'[7] Adam's first sin has brought death to all of creation and, since then, death is our cruel and powerful enemy (Gen. 3). Death for all of Adam's posterity is Adam's fault and the story of the coming of Jesus the Messiah is the Saviour's plan and the gospel message. Death, physically and spiritually, were lost to us when Adam sinned and so death passed to all creation (Rom. 5:12; Eph. 2:1). As R A Webb states, 'In the fall, the sinner not only lost the rights and the footing of a child, but He lost also the heart and the spirit of a child. That is, He lost at once His filial position and His filial nature. He now stands in need of some scheme for regaining both—His filial status and His filial spirit.'[8] Note what Webb is saying: we are all so fallen, so lost, so undone, that we are now no longer as

Adam in his original state of righteousness so sinners needing redemption. Adam stood in Eden as the representative of all humanity and his failure cost us all dear. Jesus, the Son of Man, replaces Adam as our Kinsman Redeemer (v. 22; cf. Rom. 5:1; 7:4).[9] Note also (here) how history and the gospel are inseparably liked: Adam and the Fall—Jesus and the Resurrection. They are meant to be viewed as the one (gospel) story and two gargantuan moments in the world's history. Adam's disobedience brought death and Jesus Christ's (obedience and) resurrection brings eternal life. No historical, scientific or theological alteration can be substituted for the scriptural view of two historic representatives and two historical Adams (v. 22). Jesus Christ's claim that He is 'the resurrection and the life' (John 11:25) is founded on Edenic salvific history. Adam's disobedience brought death and now there is a 'time to die' (Ecc. 3:2a). The bodily resurrection of Jesus on the third day has defeated death through 'the second Man' and now there is a time to believe:

For as in Adam all die, even so in Christ all shall be made alive. (v. 22)[10]

THE ANTICIPATION OF LIFE TO COME

Paul adds a third gigantic future historic gospel moment: the Second Coming (parousia):

But each one in His own *order*: Christ the firstfruits, afterward those *who are* Christ's at His coming. Then *comes* the end, when He delivers the kingdom to God the Father, when He puts an end to all rule and all authority and power. (vv. 23–24)

At the Second Coming there will be a set 'order' (Gk. *tagma*: a military term) to events so the prophesied future will be enacted as God has predetermined, 'each one in His own order' (v. 23), i.e. with precision and discipline in order of rank. The risen Saviour was first, then those who belong to Christ later, 'at His coming'. He rose on the third day and is now seated at the right hand of the Father in heaven (specifically the 'third' heaven; 2 Cor. 12:2). There the saints, those dead and buried, await His Second Coming. Paul excludes all unbelievers from this blessing and promise. John Murray writes: 'The resurrection of the wicked does not receive the same prominence as that of the righteous. The reason for this is that the Scriptures are mainly concerned with resurrection to life and salvation. The resurrection of Christ is cardinal in the accomplishment of salvation ... All we can say of the resurrection of the unjust is that they will be raised from the dead, that their disembodied spirits will be reunited with their bodies, that the integrity of personal life will be thus reconstituted, and that the bodies will be endowed with qualities adapted to their eternal abode.'[11]

Between 'Christ the firstfruits' and 'those who are Christ's at His coming' (v. 23) stands the ascension and heavenly session of Christ Jesus. The phrase, 'Then comes the end' indicates that time as we know it, will end and 'the new heavens and earth' will appear (Rom. 8:23; 2 Peter 3:10; Rev. 21, 22; cf. Isa. 66:22–24). He comes as regent King, personally; powerfully; triumphantly. Then the final and full harvest will be gathered in (Matt. 24:36–51).

THE ARRANGEMENT OF LIFE TO COME

The rule of Christ as Mediator holds sway while He governs His redeemed Church in secession from heaven. It is hard to fit a millennium in to this order; 'Then *comes* the end (*telos*)'. So Paul teaches here that the resurrection of the righteous is at the end of the age and will be a worldwide event. As our representative, the risen Jesus Christ, when in session, acts in the role of viceroy (one who acts in the name of another), reigning in heaven and making intercession for us (Rom. 8:34). No other religion claims, or offers or gives so much to its followers as Christianity. The resurrection day and the Second Coming of Jesus are inseparably united in the eternal plan of redemption:

For He must reign till He has put all enemies under His feet. (v. 25)

Our Mediator must reign, having dominion as God's Son and Saviour. He reigns under the covenant agreed (in the council of redemption) before time began.[12] As Messiah and Shepherd He protects and cares for His own sheep and He rules in their hearts through faith by His (Holy) Spirit (1 John 3:24). He also has dominion in the church as its head and Ruler (cf. Ps. 8:2, 6; Matt. 21:16; Col. 1:16–17; Phil. 2:9–11). Our risen Saviour possesses, 'all power and authority in heaven and on earth' (Matt. 28:18), and He will finish the work given Him to do. As the Father's viceroy, He sits and He acts in the Father's name and subdues all principalities and powers against His kingdom and bride the redeemed Church (Rom. 8:38–39; cf. Eph. 6:12). His resurrection guaranteed a golden age and a glorious rule. The language here makes it plain that Jesus Christ's ultimate victory is comprehensive, complete, decisive and permanent. His enemies will be no more and death the last enemy will be destroyed. Then all creation will once more be subject to Him:

For He must reign till He has put all enemies under His feet. The last enemy *that* will be destroyed *is* death. (vv. 25–26)

Now when all things are made subject to Him, then the Son Himself will also be subject to Him who put all things under Him, that God may be all in all. (v. 28)

When the Son's mediatorial work is accomplished, the world as we know it will end. Charles Hodge says: 'When the work of redemption has been accomplished, the dead raised, the judgment held, the enemies of Christ all subdued, then, and not till then, will the Son of God Himself be subject to Him who put all things under Him' (see v. 24).[13] As God, Jesus will reign forever, and as Mediator He will relinquish His power to the Godhead. When the work of salvation is finished there will be a change in administration and God will come into direct contact with earth but not through a mediator (Rev. 21:3; 22:3 cf. Luke 1:33; Gen. 1:31, 3:8). An enormous and eternal change is coming when, 'God will be all in all' and death will be destroyed. The gospel promised deliverance from death—the last enemy (Heb. 2:14ff)—and Jesus Christ's resurrection from the dead delivers it.

Conclusion

BAPTISM OF THE DEAD (VV. 29–34)

The practice of vicarious baptism has had many possible interpretations. Baptising the dead may have been a contemporary practice in Paul's time.[14] One can imagine it so because relatives of the deceased would want their loved ones to be in heaven too; thus this useless practice. Did the Corinthians believe in vicarious baptism? Calvin thinks so.[15] There are at least 15 explanations in extant commentaries of this practice. The most probable explanation is that whoever Paul is thinking about, those mentioned ('they' in verse 29), deny the resurrection and so He is arguing, 'so why bother with baptism?':

Otherwise, what will *they* do who are baptized for the dead, if the dead do not rise at all? Why then are they baptized for the dead? And why do we stand in jeopardy every hour? (vv. 29–30)

If Christ was not raised Paul has argued with a pastoral heart and speaks plainly: 'Do not be deceived: "Evil company corrupts good habits." Awake to righteousness, and do not sin; for some do not have the knowledge of God. I speak *this* to your shame' (vv. 33–4). Those who have been in their youth taught the truth about Jesus and His resurrection should be ashamed if they reject its reality!

It is wise to let our lives be shaped by gospel truth so that we live by faith, walk in faith and pray for the salvation of the lost. We should be burdened for sinners and unbelievers and those who reject Christ Jesus. They are on their way to hell; to the awfulness and hopelessness of eternal hell fire. We are to evangelise the unreached peoples for time is short, because, 'it is appointed for men once to die, but after this the judgment' (Heb. 9:27).

Christian hope is preached to all through the gospel of the resurrection of Jesus Christ on the third day from the dead. This is the reality; it was prophesised, it is historically witnessed and it is a certainty because:

Christ is risen from the dead, and has become the firstfruits of those who have fallen asleep. (v. 20)

NOTES

1 Morison, *Who Moved the Stone?*, p. 140.

2 1 Corinthians is Paul's second letter; the first is lost to us.

3 Morison, *Who Moved the Stone?*, p. 136.

4 See the first chapter of Paul's epistle to the Galatians for biographical details. There is a strong tradition that Paul's execution took place on the Ostian Way in Rome by order of Emperor Nero in about AD 66, soon after writing his letter to Timothy. Because he was a Roman citizen Paul was probably beheaded rather than subjected to any more prolonged and painful death.

5 https://www.christianitytoday.com/biblestudies/articles/churchhomeleadership/nicene-apostles-creeds.html

6 https://www.christianitytoday.com/biblestudies/articles/churchhomeleadership/nicene-apostles-creeds.html Lenski, 1 & 2 Corinthians, p. 663.

7 Lenski, *1 & 2 Corinthians*, p. 663.

8 R A Webb, *The Reformed Doctrine of Adoption* (Grand Rapids, MI: Eerdmans Publishing, 1947), p. 21.

9 In the book of Ruth, Boaz was a kinsman-redeemer who redeemed Ruth so they could be married. Boaz's love represents our Saviour's in type.

10 This is not a statement endorsing universalism. As all who believe in Christ 'shall be made alive' (see Eph. 2:4–10).

11 Murray, *Collected Writings*, Vol. 2, p. 411.

12 'The covenant of redemption was a transaction that involved both obligation and reward. The Son entered into a sacred agreement with the Father. He submitted himself to the obligations of that covenantal agreement. An obligation was likewise assumed by the Father—to give His Son a reward for doing the work of redemption.' https://www.ligonier.org/blog/what-covenant-redemption/

13 Hodge, *The First Epistle to the Corinthians*, p. 333.

14 The Church of the Latter Day Saints (Mormons) practices this still. But not only relatives are targeted but ancestors and strangers too! Over 7 million deceased persons have had a vicarious baptism and this includes all Roman Catholic popes and some US Presidents.

15 John Calvin, 'When anyone had been deprived of baptism by sudden death, the Corinthians were in the habit of substituting a living person for the dead one, to be baptised at His grave' (*Commentary*, p. 329). R C H Lenski seems to agree with Him (*Commentary*, p. 689).

Resurrection change (1 Cor. 15:35–58)

Christ redeemed the whole person, and thus the consummation of redemption must involve the redemption of the body (Rom. 8:23; cf. Eph. 1:14). It is in the integrity of personal life, reconstructed by resurrection, that the saints will enter into and eternally enjoy the inheritance incorruptible, undefiled, and unfading.[1]

To be like Christ in any measure is grace but to be like Christ completely is glory. (Alfred Plummer)

Some thinkers would have us believe that there was no bodily resurrection and it was a vision or hallucination sent by God to the apostles that convinced them that Jesus had risen! This denies the hope of the gospel message. In Paul's First Corinthians 15 monologue he defends the bodily resurrection and begins the second half of the chapter with two questions to be answered: (i) 'How are the dead raised up'? (ii) 'With what body do they come?' (v. 35), both questions receive a rebuke: 'Foolish one' (v. 36). Those who question this miracle need to think again! Paul now moves from the fact of the resurrection to the substance of the resurrection: from the possibility to the actuality; from the perception to the science.

Do the doubters think that bodily resurrection is impossible? They must think again for nature tells us what we can expect (v. 37). In fact, nature tells us that resurrection is on its way. Surely the words of Jesus to the disciples are pertinent here, 'O fools and slow of heart' (Luke 24:25) and Paul echoes that in the words below:

Foolish one, what you sow is not made alive unless it dies. And what you sow, you do

not sow that body that shall be, but mere grain-perhaps wheat or some other *grain*.
But God gives it a body as He pleases, and to each seed its own body. (vv. 36–8)

We ask, then, how can those martyrs burned at the stake be raised up?
Men like William Tyndale (died *c.* 1536); or how can bomb victims or
those drowned at sea and eaten by cold-blooded vertebrates (so nothing
remains) be raised up? How can people be resurrected and what will the
final glorified body look like when it has been consumed and assimilated
into another corporeal entity utterly destroyed? Surely that would be a
miracle! We answer 'Yes, it would', because the gospel promise of eternal
life has taken into account the historic miracle of Jesus Christ's
resurrection and the believer's new life hope 'in Christ'. Calvin said,
'Nothing is more repugnant to human reason than this tenet of faith. For
nobody else except God, can convince us that after our bodies, which are
subject to corruption, have rotted away or been consumed by fire or torn
to pieces by wild animals, will be returned to their wholeness, but in a far
better nature.'[2] The new resurrection body of believers is given as
designed and created by God, 'God gives it a body as He pleases' (v. 38).
We of course want to know what we will look like—how very
earth-bound and conceited! Perhaps, however, there is a clue in Jesus's
words which answers us: 'in the resurrection they neither marry nor are
given in marriage, but are like angels of God in heaven' (Matt. 22:30).
The doctrine of the resurrection is explained by Paul using three
illustrations:

1. 'Seed' (vv. 36–37); 'what you sow, you do not sow that body that
   shall be, but mere grain-perhaps wheat or some other *grain*'.
   Death is essential to life in the organic agrarian world. Thus when
   a Christian is burned at the stake or their remains buried and
   covered with earth the body is *sown* to await the day of
   resurrection. However, God has a wonderful surprise waiting for
   His people on the resurrection day; there is continuity between

seed sown and plant grown. The future body will not be like the present one but an enduring likeness will persist although we cannot tell its eternal outward manifestation.

2. 'Flesh' (v. 39); 'All flesh *is* not the same flesh, but *there is* one *kind of* flesh of men, another flesh of animals, another of fish, *and* another of birds.' God has made men and animals with different *flesh* (Gk. *sarx*, 'physical body'—corruptible and weak). This debunks evolutionary theory—old or new. The biblical 'kinds' of Genesis 1 and 2 are separate families (genus), 'there is one kind of flesh of men, another flesh of animals'. Men and beasts are different and are clearly seen to be so. If we say otherwise because of evolutionary hypothesis, we conclude that Paul and Genesis 1 and 2 are in error as to the origins of the human race. This unbiblical conclusion would invalidate the Bible doctrine of a physical resurrection as argued here by Paul and spoken of in the Gospels (Mark 16:12). That would be very serious indeed to the Christian message and its theology but Paul is using this illustration as a prime example and explanation for believing in the resurrection.

3. 'Celestial and terrestrial bodies' (v. 40); 'the glory of the celestial *is* one, and the *glory* of the terrestrial *is* another'. These have unequal *glory*, i.e. one is 'star [gaseous] like' and the other is 'tree [organic] like'. There is even a difference in heavenly bodies, 'There is one glory of the sun, another glory of the moon, and another glory of the stars; for one star differs from another star in glory' (v. 41). This may indicate that at the resurrection different saints will have different degrees of honour and glory without violating the biblical promises of Matthew 22:30 and 1 John 3:1–2.

From these three illustrations Paul offers us hope for life to come (vv. 42–4):

- '*The body* is sown in corruption, it is raised in incorruption.'

- 'It is sown in dishonour, it is raised in glory.'
- 'It is sown in weakness, it is raised in power.'
- 'It is sown a natural body, it is raised a spiritual body. There is a natural body, and there is a spiritual body.'

Four conclusions

Paul has four conclusions that clarify for us the nature and substance of eternal resurrection existence informing us that our final eternal (third) state will be beyond and above all human reckoning (vv. 42–49).[3] From these verses we see:

1. Death is the corruption of the flesh but resurrection is incorruption (v. 42): '*The body* is sown in corruption, it is raised in incorruption.' Christ will change our body of humiliation and make it like His glorified body full of eternal promise with no flaws. An undying existence is what is promised. Our origin in Adam is fixed and we resemble him (he is the progenitor) and will die, but our destiny in Christ is also fixed by election, grace and the new birth leading to the promise of resurrection.

2. Death is dishonour but resurrection is honour and glory (v. 43a): 'It is sown in dishonour, it is raised in glory.' The bereaved put the best clothes on their dead loved ones and place them in a fine casket topped with flowers to bestow honour upon them, but death is dishonour; the Fall has seen to that (Gen. 3). Conversely, those who partake in Christ's resurrection are promised power without weakness and honour without shame. Lenski notes, 'In this life the ordinary animations of our body continue even though we are spiritually re-born, but in the resurrection, the spirit takes complete control of the body, (which has been gloriously refashioned) so as to respond fully to that control.'[4]

3. Death is weakness but resurrection is a powerful life (v. 43b): 'It is sown in weakness, it is raised in power.' Weakness leads to death

as our ability to cope runs out and when we die we decay in the grave but resurrection provides strength and vitality and glory. The natural body needs food, sleep and water but the new body will have no need of these things for the Spirit dominates, controls and gives life which flows from the throne of God (Rev. 22:1ff). At present we know weakness, now we know in part, now by faith spirituality begins, but then the power of an endless life arrives. Then obedience will be perfect, 'as it is in heaven' among the holy elect angels (Matt. 6:10b).

4. Death is natural but resurrection is spiritual (v. 44): 'It is sown a natural body, it is raised a spiritual body. There is a natural body, and there is a spiritual body'. Paul explains this more fully in his epistle to the Philippians, 'the Lord Jesus Christ, who will transform our lowly body that it may be conformed to His glorious body, according to the working by which He is able even to subdue all things to Himself' (3:20b–21). The Spirit revives those deceased and animates their body. When life is taken from us the body becomes lifeless and cold. However, the cold and decayed body that lies in the earth will live again when it is given a 'spiritual' lift. It is the same body but has different qualities: 'He however does not describe a bodiless resurrection. We will not be ghosts but it will be new and "in all respects a proper organ for the Spirit" ... Then the Spirit will dominate completely and we will be controlled by the Holy Spirit.'[5]

Paul has explained what believers are to look forward to with assurance and anticipation. Dear reader, believe in it; wait for it and rejoice because of it! Your future state will be something very, very special indeed. Death is an unpleasant smell (John 11:39) but resurrection is sweet to the taste and stunning in glory. This is because our new body is from heaven and speaks about the difference between the 'now' and the 'not yet'.

Adam and Christ Jesus

In verses 45–46 Paul, still deals with the enquiry, 'with what body do they come?' (v. 35b), and he feels that it is important to add another illustration to answer this question by means of Adam and Christ Jesus:

And so it is written, 'The first man Adam became a living being. The last Adam *became* a life-giving spirit,' explaining that, 'the spiritual is not first, but the natural, and afterward the spiritual.' (vv. 45–46)

We are firstly reminded that the eternal state (in the new heavens and earth) will be so very different than it is for us *now* on this fallen world, just as the present existence is different from that perfect state of Adam and Eve's in Eden. So the new creation will be another new 'Eden' with new bodies which cannot be spoiled by sin or Satan. Also, see the contrasted continuity between the 'first man [who] *was* of the earth, *made* of dust; the second Man [who] *is* the Lord from heaven' (v. 47), confirming that Adam was made from the dust of the earth by a miraculous instant creation and that those in Christ will 'bear the image of the heavenly *Man*' (Gk. 'bear' = *phoreo*, 'I carry' or 'I wear'; and 'image' = *eikov*, 'it always supposes a prototype, from what it is drawn'. It is used of the Monarch's head on a coin).[6]

We will 'wear' a resurrected Christ likeness because we will be like Him (1 John 3:1–2). When cross-referenced with Romans chapter 5 we see that Adam was 'a type (topos = a pattern/figure) of Him who was to come' (v. 14b). The first, 'the *man* of dust' was disobedient and sin entered the creation but 'the heavenly *Man*' was obedient unto death and 'many will be made righteous' (v. 19). Or as here:

As *was* the *man* of dust, so also *are* those *who are made* of dust; and as *is* the heavenly *Man*, so also *are* those *who are* heavenly. And as we have borne the image of the man of dust, we shall also bear the image of the heavenly *Man*. (vv. 48–49)

What we have here is not philosophy but rather theomacy and biblical eschatology. We see that Paul get his doctrine from Old Testament (Gen. 2:7; Isa. 64:4; 65:17).[7]

Final victory (vv. 50–57)

Paul is answering the obvious questions, what will happen to those who are alive when Jesus Christ returns? Will they have a part in the resurrection too? He introduces his short but glorious answer with concluding remarks which bring to us one of the most wonderful statements in Paul's theological corpus:

> Now this I say, brethren, that flesh and blood cannot inherit the kingdom of God; nor does corruption inherit incorruption. (v. 50)

This has echoes of repetition (as all concluding remarks do) but it confers inspirational hope, notice:

(1) IT IS A *PROPHESIED* CHANGE (VV. 51–52A)

Having reviewed the evidence for the bodily resurrection of Jesus the Messiah (cited above) Paul adds to it His own testimony of conclusion and personal assurance, 'Behold, I tell you a mystery. We shall not all sleep, but we shall all be changed—in a moment, in the twinkling of an eye, at the last trumpet' (vv. 51–52).[8] In this context, 'sleep' is a euphemism for death and equivalent to 'die': 'we shall not all die', 'but we shall all be changed' (Gk. *allassw*), is 'to transform', and here 'to make other than it is'. This will happen 'In a moment' (Gk. *atomo*; that is, time is so short as to be incapable of further division). This disagrees with evolution theory that believes it takes long, long ages for (*nephesh*) flesh to change. This means that there will be no time left on the day of Judgement Day to change your mind, or repent or say sorry, because in a millisecond 'at the twinkling of an eye' (Gk. *hripe*; a flicker or a quiver; as fast as that) 'We shall all be changed'![9]

(2) IT IS A *PUBLIC* CHANGE (VV. 52B–55)

Our new bodies as described above by Paul will be so changed they will no longer be subject to the laws of nature or physical change: 'For the trumpet will sound, and the dead will be raised incorruptible, and we shall be changed' (v. 52b). The resurrection will happen when the last trumpet sounds. In the book of the Revelation seven trumpets sound (Rev. 8:7, 9, 11; 13: 9:12; 14:11:14). When the *last* resonates at the close of the age, 'the Lord Himself will descend from heaven with a shout, with the voice of an archangel, and with the trumpet of God. And the dead in Christ will rise first' (1 Thess. 4:16). This indicates that at His coming Jesus returns to earth publicly for 'every eye shall see Him' (Matt. 24:27, 31) demonstrating that He is Lord of the living and the dead and Lord of heaven and earth. It is needful to take Jesus's warning from the parable of the *Wise and Foolish Virgins*, five of whom at the Bridegroom's coming (again), are refused access to the marriage supper of the Lamb (Matt. 25:1-13; Rev. 19:19). However, this will not be the outcome for those who have faith in Christ's return and hold their lamps trimmed and full of oil (Matt. 25:1–13; Rev. 19:19). They will 'put on incorruption' and 'put on immortality' and 'be conformed to His (Christ's) glorious body' at His coming (Phil. 3:21). Their 'lowly bodies' which are unfit for heaven will be transformed and become robust for an eternal existence with God and the holy angels:

> For this corruptible must put on incorruption, and this mortal must put on immortality. So when this corruptible has put on incorruption, and this mortal has put on immortality, then shall be brought to pass the saying that is written: '*Death is swallowed up in victory.*' (vv. 53–54)

As Paul continues he is still answering the obvious question, 'What will happen to those who are alive when Jesus Christ returns; will they have a part in the resurrection too?' The resurrection guarantees something special; Paul was first changed by conversion but he will be changed *again* by resurrection. In the eternal state we ever remain perfect and by immortality we are ever free from the power of death ever again. The moment of immortality is an instant act (as the Gk. *aorist* tense indicates) that will be both transforming inside and outside.

Paul, quoting Hosea 13:14, says, 'O Death, where is your sting? O Hades, where is your victory?' (v. 55; cf. Isa. 25:8). Death is swallowed up and disappears and is no more known. Luther said, 'One death, devoured the others.'[10] No further traces of age, infirmity and death will be found and sufferings of this present time will finish. The expectation of the creation that eagerly waits for the revealing of the sons of God will be known. The bondage of corruption will be gone and the glorious liberty of the children of God with our adoption and the redemption of our body will be complete (Rom. 8:18–23). What looked like a permanent victory for death and decay is overturned and swallowed up for 'there's victory in Jesus our Saviour forever'. What superlatives! What victory! What prospect is now contemplated?

O Death, where is your sting? O Hades, where is your victory? (v. 55)

(3) IT IS A BETTER AND PLEASANT CHANGE (VV. 56–57)

Corruption will put on incorruption and the mortal the immortal and there will be a 'transforming' and also a 'conforming' at the resurrection because we shall be like Him (1 John 3:1–2) and we will sin no more, Hallelujah! We will have a new body and a new state. We will have a new humanity and there will be a new earth free from sin and without Satan. Now conformed unto the likeness of the risen Saviour we shall be unable to sin and Jesus's impeccability will be shared with us.[11] The incarnate God-man was, 'not able to sin' and being wholly transformed all the saints will be conformed to the Saviour's resurrection heavenly likeness which secures for eternity a holy re-creation (Phil. 3:20b–21:; 1 John 3:1).[12]

From dust and ashes we will arise. We shall be forever changed to give praise to God and His Christ: it is pleasant and predestined. Worship and service is the destiny of all those in Christ Jesus and His death and resurrection bought it for us. The 'self' (*ego*) and the flesh (*sarx*) and the dominion of sin will vanish and the 'Jesus only' reality will have begun, 'Thanks be to God, who gives us the victory through our Lord Jesus Christ' (v. 57). The Revelation of John pictures this hope:

And there shall be no more curse, but the throne of God and of the Lamb shall be in it, and His servants shall serve Him. They shall see His face, and His name *shall be* on their foreheads. There shall be no night there: They need no lamp nor light of the sun, for the Lord God gives them light. And they shall reign forever and ever. (Rev. 22:3–5)

Through, by and in worship the saints shall find their eternal destiny and serve God in the new heavens and new earth. There with their Saviour they will be fulfilled as Adam and Eve were meant to be in the Garden of Eden and more.

Conclusion

Divine foreknowledge is an anchor for the soul and God's purpose is to conform us to the firstborn Redeemer. His resurrection assures us of our guaranteed future and glorification is already accomplished. As the firstborn, Jesus Christ, through resurrection from death, is the prototype of the promise to come (Rev. 1:5):

He also predestined *to be* conformed to the image of His Son, that He might be the firstborn among many brethren. (Rom. 8:29)

To be *predestined* is to be loved and chosen before the foundation of the world. Adoption and redemption are integrally related (Eph. 1:5). Thus adoption reminds us of our predestination. As Hodge puts it, 'Election is the cause or source of all subsequent benefits.'[13] Predestination tells us that God had a plan: which means to 'determine beforehand'. What did God predetermine? To transform His elect by resurrection to be conformed to the image of His Son. To be *conformed* (Gk. a transformation that revolutionises appearance in mind and life and in complete harmony with Christ's resurrected existence).[14] As we have seen above, it is a transformation through resurrection in the likeness of the risen Jesus Christ. When it comes to the cross with its pain and humiliations we must remember that 'God allows what He hates to accomplish what He loves' so it is that saints through resurrection conform to Jesus Christ's impeccable likeness.[15] Our eternal sonship is the goal of resurrection. We are 'predestined *to be* conformed to the image of His Son, that He might be the firstborn among many brethren ... these He also glorified' (Rom. 8:29, 30b). Here is the chief end of the predestination, and what is last in execution was first in intention.

Can we accept Paul's teaching as from God the Spirit? Paul speaks by revelation and inspiration—'Revelation [which the prophets had from God] makes truth known, and inspiration provides for its infallible recording.'[16] Without the revealed mysteries Paul speaks of we would be still in the dark and walk blindly (1 Cor. 2:7; Eph. 5:32; 2 Thess. 2:7; cf. Matt. 23:24; Luke 6:39). Paul preaches that a momentous change is coming and all things will change for the better. We know that this present age has a predetermined and time-limited existence (Matt. 28:20). By the Holy Spirit's revelation through Paul we now know that all Christians 'shall not all sleep, but we shall all be changed in a moment, in the twinkling of an eye, at the last trumpet' (vv. 51–52). The phrase, 'We shall all be changed' (v. 51a) reminds us that time is short for all of us. Paul prophesies here that at the end time the resurrection reality will not be by evolution or artificial intelligence, magic or hocus-pocus, but by the miraculous work of Almighty God when, in an infinitesimal moment, we shall all be changed into Christ's likeness: the, 'body we bury remains buried, whatever it is that arises is something else'.[17]

What did Paul mean when he said, 'He rose again the third day according to the Scriptures' (1 Cor. 15:4)? He infers that the physical bodily resurrection of Jesus is most powerful in stimulating persevering zeal in those who believe, 'Therefore, my beloved brethren, be steadfast, immovable, always abounding in the work of the Lord, knowing that your labour is not in vain' (v. 58). Paul's aim in writing was to correct those in error on this very important subject, thus his thoughtful and detailed monologue. If the resurrection is a lie then there would be cataclysmic consequences affecting Christian doctrine and practice in the churches and the world.

NOTES

1 Murray, Vol. 2, *Collected Writings*, p. 412.

2 John Calvin, *1 Corinthians Commentary* (Grand Rapids, MI: W B Eerdmans Publishing, 1996), p. 335.

3 See Chapter 7 above.

4 Lenski, *1 & 2 Corinthians*, p. 723.

5 Ibid. pp. 714, 723.

6 R C Trench, *Synonyms of the New Testament* (Grand Rapids, MI: W B Eerdmans Publishing, 1976).

7 *Theomancy* (Gr *theomanteiā* spirit of prophecy); a person directly inspired immediately by the Spirit of God. cf., *The Chambers Dictionary* 2003; *The Chambers Thesaurus* 2004; (Chambers Harrap Publishers Ltd).

8 'Mystery' (Gk, *mustérion*, 'a secret now revealed once hidden').

9 'Nephesh' flesh, see Gen. 1–2.

10 Ibid. Lenski, p. 747.

11 It means 'not liable to sin' and comes from the Latin word *impeccabilis*.

12 For the impeccability of Jesus Christ and its implications for our redemption, see my, *The Real Lord's Prayer* (Day One Publications, 2012), pp. 73–78.

13 Hodge, *The Epistle to the Ephesians*, p. 29.

14 'The morphe may be assumed the essence of a thing', R C Trench (Grand Rapids, MI: W B Eerdmans, 1976), p. 265.

15 https://www.goodreads.com/quotes/12065-sometimes-god-allows-what-he-hates-to-accomplish-what-he

16 J Barton Payne, *The Theology of the Older Testament* (Grand Rapids, MI; Zondervan Publishing, 1972), p. 63.

17 Lenski, *1 & 2 Corinthians*, p. 731.

Chapter 14

Resurrection day

The bodies of the unjust shall, by the power of Christ, be raised to dishonour; the bodies of the just, by His Spirit, unto honour, and be made conformable to His own glorious body. (Westminster Confession of Faith)[1]

The resurrection is a proclamation of what? ... it is the proclamation of the fact that the world is to be judged in righteousness, that the wrath of God is to be revealed against all ungodliness and unrighteousness of men, and that Christ is the Judge. The resurrection is a declaration, therefore, of this tremendous doctrine of the wrath of God. (Dr Martyn Lloyd-Jones)[2]

In the plan of redemption the cross of Jesus Christ brought adoption and filial grace while the resurrection brings transformation and conformation unto the likeness of Christ Jesus glorified (1 Cor. 15:47–49). The traditional Christian view of the resurrection of redeemed saints made possible by Jesus Christ's own resurrection on the third day is that they are promised God's Spirit of adoption by which God makes them His children, with all the rights of sonship. This relationship was bought by the precious blood of Jesus Christ on Calvary and sealed by the Holy Spirit:

Having predestined us to adoption as sons by Jesus Christ to Himself ... He made us accepted in the Beloved. In Him we have redemption through His blood, the forgiveness of sins. (Eph. 2:5, 7)

This adoption by God is immediate on justification by faith alone (1 John 1:12–13). It bestows a new dignity and the promises of a (present) salvation and (a future) glory with God as His children and joint heirs with Christ (Gal. 4:6; Rom. 8:23). S B Ferguson says, 'Sonship has a retrospective and a prospective dimension. It recognises what has already been accomplished, but it also recognises that there is still more to come.'[3] The believer's dignity and destiny both are promised because of adoption. This indicates that the present blessings of the children of God are a foretaste of what lies ahead. The epistle of Paul to the Romans, written c. AD 57, encourages perseverance as well as hope while Christians await the Second Coming of Jesus Christ:

We also who have the firstfruits of the Spirit, even we ourselves groan within ourselves, eagerly waiting for the adoption, the redemption of our body. (Rom. 8:23)

Had the Saviour never come forth from the grave we could never be sure that His work of vicarious atonement had been fully successful. Had Jesus not risen from the conflict with the last enemy (death) we could not be certain that Satan, who had the power of death, was defeated; as the epistle to the Hebrews reports, 'that through death He might destroy Him that had the power of death' (Heb. 2:14).

The resurrection of the body

In the first epistle of John there is a stress on the resurrection promised to God's children in Christ and its transforming power. Bodily resurrection and the Second Coming of Jesus are inseparably united in the eternal plan of redemption. This is often described as the 'general resurrection'. The words of committal, which are often used at the grave side by the clergy, make this point:

For as much as it has pleased almighty God to take the soul of our *brother* departed, we here commit *his* body to the ground, earth to earth, ashes to ashes, dust to dust, to await the general resurrection at the last day, through Jesus Christ our Lord.[4]

It is only the born again children of God who will walk the streets of gold because regeneration precedes bodily resurrection before Christ's

Second Advent (John 3:3). Those in the grave will rise and those still alive will, at the last trumpet blast, be raised incorruptible (1 Thess. 3:13b; 4:16–17; cf. 1 Cor. 6:13).

The redeemed children of the Father are glorified in the risen and ascended Christ Jesus. Having transferred us from the kingdom of darkness into the kingdom of His dear Son, the adopted people of God are predestined for eternal glory with Him. This is seen clearly in Paul's epistles but also in 1 John chapter 3. Both convey this anticipated glory to come. This glory is not ours on our own account but by reason of Jesus's cross-work and our union with Him through faith: 'He has delivered us from the power of darkness and conveyed *us* into the kingdom of the Son of His love' (Col. 1:13). Paul's eyes were always fixed on redemption glory at the end of the age, which replaces the humiliation of sin and the fall. Then, the present foretaste of heaven in the soul will be replaced with 'the glory which shall be revealed in us' as joint heirs with Him. For John, the joy of future glorification together with Christ Jesus is the result of the reality of the love of God the Father through Jesus Christ the Son to unworthy sinners. This something to 'behold' (1 John 3:1), suggests that we reflect on the cost of the death of his Son. John, overcome with God's true love and the hope of anticipated Christ likeness at the last day, said:

Behold what manner of love the Father has bestowed on us, that we should be called children of God! Therefore the world does not know us, because it did not know Him. Beloved, now we are children of God; and it has not yet been revealed what we shall be, but we know that when He is revealed, we shall be like Him, for we shall see Him as He is. (1 John 3:1–2)

The ascension not only took Jesus to heaven but it secured our place in heaven with Him.[5] When He left this world, Jesus did not forget the sheep for which He died. The reigning, loving Christ Jesus is preparing (i.e.

securing) a place, 'a mansion' (Gk. *mone*, 'dwelling place'), for all the people of God so they can be with Him forever (John 14:1–2). In heavenly session, our coming King fulfils the sweet promise that He will never leave them or forsake them (Matt. 28:20b).[6] At death, He will bring all the people of God to 'Paradise' the moment they breathe their last and leave the world.[7] Thus there will be room for all those who, by faith in the gospel, have prepared themselves to be with Him. The separation of soul and body (death) is the signal to Jesus to send heavenly [holy] angels to bring the redeemed to His side so that they are with Him in the intermediate state (Luke 16:22; 2 Cor. 5:1–8). At the resurrection of the just on the last day, the dead in Christ will be raised and be forever with the Lord (1 Thess. 4:16–18). The risen and ascended Jesus Christ is the forerunner who brings hope and eternal redemption 'for us' (Heb. 4:20; 9:12). This was the joy set before Him (Heb. 12:2). This was the plan which was prepared in eternity: 'before the foundation of the world' (Matt. 25:34; 1 Peter 1:20).

The Second Coming[8]

Teaching on the Second Coming of Jesus Christ finds expression throughout the New Testament. If one should read it from cover to cover then it will be seen that the New Testament believes in a time-changing future event. In the book of the Revelation we have it predicted:

Behold, He is coming with clouds, and every eye shall see Him and they also who pierced Him. And all the tribes of the earth shall mourn because of Him. Even so, Amen. (Rev. 1:7)

This conviction is well-established in the Old Testament which point to the day of the Lord's coming (Ps. 2:6–8; Dan. 7:13–14; Isa. 65:17; cf. Acts 13:33). The church has always loved this teaching because it brings promise, encouragement, hope and comfort to the adopted children of God. For the

New Testament, the Second Advent of Christ is described also as 'the day of the Lord' (1 Thess. 5:2) and it points us forward to the end of time as we know it and that moment in history when God shall vindicate His resurrected Son's first advent and vicarious atonement (Phil. 2:9–11). The saints who were martyred, despised and regarded as an enigma by unbelievers throughout the centuries will be revealed to the universe as God's adopted children (Rom. 8:18–23). They will be glorified with their Saviour and they will be forever with Him in His resurrection glory. When thinking about the Second Coming in three stages and it is helpful to ask: (i) what events are prior to Christ's coming, (ii) what events are planned at Christ's coming and, (iii) what is proposed after Christ's coming? This allows one to see the 'big picture'. The events planned at the Second Advent of the Saviour are articulated in the words, 'The Lord *Himself* will descend from heaven with a shout' (1 Thess. 4: 16). Christians expect a personal and visible return of the Lord Jesus Christ: 'when the Lord is revealed from heaven with His mighty angels' (Mark 13:24–27). The Greek word (*parousia*) translated 'coming' is also happily translated 'presence', so when Christ himself comes He will be present with us, 'He comes, in that Day, to be glorified in His saints and to be admired among all those who believe' (2 Thess. 1:10a). This coming presence will be powerful and awesome: 'In flaming fire taking vengeance on those who do not know God' (2 Thess. 1:8). These strong words are apt to put us off if we do not accept the Bible as wholly reliable. Yet these verses speak of a faith that witnesses to the testimony of the early church. Only in the Bible do we learn of the things that are to come and only in the Bible can we learn how to flee from the wrath to come (Rev. 19:11–16). The Second Advent will bring the Lord Jesus Christ from heaven. He will return with His angels (Matt. 13:30, 41; 24:31); the earth with be burned up in a worldwide conflagration and the wicked judged (2 Pet. 3:10–13). Those who will be judged are described as, 'those who do not know God' (2 Thess. 1:8). Having remained unrepentant all their lives they are lost forever. The justified people of God will share in Christ's victory by believing that He is, 'the resurrection and the life' (John 11:25–26). When the resurrection day arrives believers will be given a body like the risen Saviour's; it shall be perfect, fitted for a spiritual existence and it will have the power of an endless life and they will share in Christ's victory (1 Cor. 15:50–55).

Waiting for Jesus to come

Peter preached a future resurrection of the just as a gift of faith through grace still to come, 'rest your hope fully upon the grace that is to be brought to you at the revelation of Jesus Christ' (1 Pet. 1:3–4, 13). God's work, of free grace also embraces the final moment when the adopted children of God are raised from the dead, 'at the revelation of Jesus Christ' (Gk. *apocalypsis*, 'an unveiling'). 'The assurance of Christ's return is held out as a compelling motive for endurance through the storms and tribulations of life.'[9] Optimism inspiring hope in God is the fruit of faith in God's risen Son, Jesus Christ.

Paul ends his First Corinthians chapter 15 monologue by adding a conclusion that is practical and meant to lead to perseverance by the adopted people of God. He says, 'I have taught you about the future and the glory to come that is yours in Christ our Saviour. Your response is to walk by faith and not by sight and to give ourselves to ministry and good works until He comes again' and then he calls also for patience and hope in bodily resurrection:

Therefore, my beloved brethren, be steadfast, immovable, always abounding in the work of the Lord, knowing that your labour is not in vain in the Lord. (v. 58)

Notice:

1. PAUL'S LOVING EXCLAMATION: 'MY BELOVED BRETHREN'.

An exclamation is a bold or sharp cry, emotional utterance or outburst: 'Therefore'; because of the evidences, the theological explanation given and the practical results of Christ's resurrection, he now adds a practical application. Paul has a pastor's heart. He meant what he said! He desired their good. He loved them warmly. This is the pastor's heart revealed and the servant's motivation clarified. Any other motive will not do! This love is not to be hidden. It was the Corinthians he loved—those awkward and disobedient people of God! Faction torn and self-willed, yet they were Christ's Church (in local sight) those for whom He died and whom Paul served. This is an example of love in action in obedience to Jesus's command that we should love one another as He loved us (John 13:34–35). This kindness and forgiveness is not dependent on God's adopted children, 'toeing the party line', or on them being super spiritual or biblically correct in every doctrine or mature in all graces. No! We are asked to love one another at all times and our prejudices or principles are not to get in the way (1 Cor. 13:4–7). He acknowledges the Corinthian believers as Christians even though they had so many faults and failings. The sanctifying Spirit of God was still at work in them.

2. PAUL'S LOVING EXHORTATION: 'BE STEADFAST IMMOVABLE, ALWAYS ABOUNDING IN THE WORK OF THE LORD'.

He wants them to be active in evangelism and service; using their gifts and showing their graces in Christ in an approach that is steadfast (Gk. *hedraioi* = strong, firm, stable—it means not shaken or agitated but confident in God's will). This is not about self-assertiveness but a holding of hope in Christ with trust and determination (cf. Eph. 6:10). So whatever life and providence throws at us he says *'be immovable'* (NIV *'Let nothing move you'*). It is a similar word to 'steadfast' so there is a double thrust. Note the *'always'*, i.e. continue and persevere and just not sometimes or most times but all the time: *'always abounding'* is the watchword in days of small things and times of apostasy in the country and in the churches. It suggests an overflow of effort and an increase of service by going the second mile (Col. 1:23). Our usefulness in the Lord's kingdom depends on how much we love and obey and persevere in the faith. Our ministries may change, our opponents may vary, but we are to trust God at all times and let our love for the Lord Jesus keep us 'redeeming the time' (Eph. 5:16).

3. PAUL'S LOVING ENCOURAGEMENT: 'KNOWING THAT YOUR LABOUR IS NOT IN VAIN IN THE LORD'.

What we do for Jesus is not in vain, nor empty, nor is it ignored by our Saviour. To 'labour' for Jesus is not wasted (Gk. *kopos*, i.e. with effort, and energy, and in weariness, and fatigue: the verb, 'I grow weary'). In fact we will in the future wish we had given Him more! Know that He sees all we do for His church and His glory. What we do is to be 'as unto Him' (Col. 3:23) and not for self but for His glory and His kingdom. This is achieved when we take up our cross and follow Him. We should ask ourselves, 'Do I labour in His harvest fields with self-sacrifice and hope?'

'The First and the Last'

The Book of the Revelation, written while John was exiled on Patmos (AD *c.* 96), proclaims Jesus's resurrection as gospel truth fixed in history and announced as hope for all who believe: 'Jesus Christ, the faithful witness, the firstborn from the dead' together with Jesus's personal witness that 'I am He who lives, and was dead, and behold, I am alive forevermore. Amen' (Rev. 1:5, 18). John elaborates on this theme linking it with the end-times while proclaiming hope to the church militant through troubled times:

To him who overcomes I will grant to sit with Me on My throne, as I also overcame and sat down with My Father on His throne. (Rev. 3:21)

John's thoughts and phrases throughout are written in apocalyptic language, thus he speaks of 'the second death', 'the morning star' and 'the souls of those who had been beheaded for their witness to Jesus and for the word of God', all to aid an understanding of the assured hope given to believers by the Spirit of God. At length, John offers a firm foundation of hope for those who were partakers in 'the first resurrection' and are at present in the Intermediate State. They will not experience the 'second death' (Rev. 2:11, 29) 'but they shall be priests of God and of Christ, and shall reign with Him a thousand years' (Rev. 20:5–6).[10]

The 'second death' refers to the experience of eternal death in the *lake of fire* following *physical death* and the decay of the body. Revelation 20:6 reveals that the first resurrection saves us from the second death. This then can be understood as the new birth; i.e. being *born again* or *born of God* (John 3:3; 1 John 3:3). This is to become alive to God and made new in Christ. We say this because a sound rule in the interpretation of Scripture is that obscure passages should be explained by the plain. Clear teaching portions of Scripture are important in explaining the symbolic and prophetic parts. Also, the Bible speaks of a spiritual as well as literal resurrection; as sinners we are, 'dead in trespasses and sins' but by faith are quickened and raised to life in Christ Jesus:

And you *He made alive*, who were dead in trespasses and sins. (Eph. 2:1)

According to Revelation 2:11 and 20:6, those who overcome the devil's attacks by being in Christ and persevering in the faith will not experience the second death. Revelation 21:8 identifies the second death with the *lake of fire*:

But the cowardly, the faithless, the polluted, the murderers, the fornicators, the sorcerers, the idolaters, and all liars, their place will be in the lake that burns with fire and sulphur, which is the *second death*.

Another reference to the resurrection hope designates Jesus with a qualifying determiner, 'These things say the First and the Last, who was dead, and came to life' (Rev. 2:8). This is the third reference to the miracle of resurrection and it is only two and a half chapters since the book opened! John's vision of the risen Jesus of Nazareth produced fear and awe: 'And when I saw Him, I fell at His feet as dead.' However, He was reassured of Christ's love when, 'He laid His right hand on me, saying to me, "Do not be afraid; I am the First and the Last"' (Rev. 1:17–18).

This moment (in John's experience) confirmed what He had already known; that His Saviour was alive and well in His glorified body (Luke 24:46; John 20:21; Acts 1:8).

Jesus proclaims himself, 'I am the Alpha and the Omega, *the* Beginning and *the* End ... who is and who was and who is to come, the Almighty ... I am the Alpha and the Omega, the First and the Last' (Rev. 1:8, 11). Thus declaring himself as 'The First Place' or 'The Ruler' of God's creation. In fact, the Greek phrase (in this verse) can be translated in a more active sense to read, 'The One who begins the creation of God', not meaning that Jesus is the first being that God created, but rather that He is the originator of the creation of God, both material and spiritual. He was not created but, rather, He began all creation. It does not say that He *had* a beginning, but that He is the Beginning. He is the *Origin* of the creation of God and He is pre-eminent over all creation. He is the Potter and we are the clay. Most commentators regard the six verses (Rev. 1:15–20) as an early hymn in honour of Christ.[11]

Revelation (2:8), the ascended Christ presents Himself as the Eternal One. Ancient Smyrna was founded *c*. 1,100 BC. Christ however, is 'older' than Smyrna. He is before time began. He is outside time. He is always and altogether God and the second person of the Trinity co-equal in the Godhead. He designates as *The First and the Last*: Smyrna may have boasted of its age and expect to survive another millennium, but when time ceases to be Jesus Christ will still the Lord of heaven. From everlasting to everlasting He is God. By timeless nature Jesus is the Son from all eternity but not by creation or inheritance. He was always the only begotten of the Father and He is that, *which was dead and is alive*. His is the Saviour of the soul and the Redeemer of the body. Resurrection victory was His. He took our guilt and, at Calvary, paid the price of our forgiveness. Thus:

The cross is vacant
The tomb is empty
The throne is occupied.

Jesus Christ overcame death and re-entered life and now reigns in Heaven. Some day we will be there with Him and shall be like Him (1 John 3:2). He is the Vanguard:
- He is first in *time*: Christ was raised as the firstfruits and His saints shall follow Him into heaven.
- He is first in *kind*: all the harvest is of the same seed and therefore the alike in impeccable holiness.
- He is first in *pledge*: His resurrection is the promise of ours to come.

This hope already rests in the heart of the believer, 'We also who have the firstfruits of the Spirit, even we ourselves groan within ourselves, eagerly waiting for the adoption, the redemption of our body' (Rom. 8:23). Here is the pledge that assures us that in Christ we will rise as He promised.

The Amen

The title of Christ as 'the Amen' (Rev. 3:14) is one of the 144 names and titles given the Jesus Christ, God's Son and Saviour in the Bible:

These things says the Amen, the Faithful and True Witness, the Beginning of the creation of God. (Rev. 3:14)

The word 'Amen' is of Hebrew origin. The word was imported into the Greek of the early Church. From Greek (*amen*) it entered into Latin and then into English as well as other European languages. It is also used in worship to affirm an address, a psalm or a prayer; as for instance, one might say, 'Amen to that!' The word *amen*, ('so be it; truly') is a declaration of affirmation translated normally as: 'verily', and 'truly'. There are fifty-two *amen's* in the Synoptic Gospels and twenty-five in John. The uses of *amen* ('verily' or 'truly') in the Gospels is special and often lacks any backward reference. Jesus used the word to affirm His own utterances, not those of another person, and the use of *amen* (single or double in form), to introduce solemn statements of Jesus in the Gospels. It had no parallel in Jewish practice.[12] *Amen* concludes the New Testament in Rev. 22:20–21.

This title of Christ as, 'the Amen' is very interesting and powerful and of significant importance. It reveals Him as the embodiment of faithfulness and truth, and the one who guarantees and fulfils the promises of God. In Isaiah 65:16 the Lord God is called the God of truth; however, in the original Hebrew, 'The God of amen.' Thus Isaiah is saying that the Lord God is the One who remains eternally true, the One who can always be relied upon. Our Lord Jesus Christ is eternally true and reliable. These are remarkable words, involving both His deity and His perfect humanity. Paul, too, is convinced that Jesus Christ is the divine Amen. In a doxology in the epistle to the Romans he so obviously applies it to the Lord Jesus who, 'according to the flesh, Christ *came*, who is over all, *the* eternally blessed God. Amen. (Rom. 9:5b).

Conclusion

The resurrection of Jesus Christ shines out of the darkness of unbelief and false religion bringing the true Light into view. The utter significance of the resurrection miracle and its relevance to Christian worship brought a change of the Sabbath day from the last to the first day of the week. Gathering on the first day of the week to worship the risen Lord of the churches is a powerful and public testimony to the truth that, 'He is risen indeed'.

Salvation

Salvation comes as a result of Christ's atoning death *and* His resurrection from the dead, sealing the work of redemption in us. This is firstly a subjective transformation (the gift spoken of to Nicodemus in John 3:3, called 'the new birth') securing to us 'a living hope' offered to all in the gospel:

[Our] Lord Jesus Christ, who according to His abundant mercy has begotten us again to a living hope through the resurrection of Jesus Christ from the dead, to an inheritance incorruptible and undefiled and that does not fade away, reserved in heaven for you, who are kept by the power of God through faith for salvation ready to be revealed in the last time. (1 Pet. 1:3–5)

The revealing 'in the last time' speaks of the Second Coming and Judgement Day. Our eternal inheritance has been secured for us by Jesus's resurrection and is now preserved (kept) for us in heaven. Our resurrection bodies are waiting 'to be revealed' (Gk. *apokalupses*, 'uncovered'). At the end of time our risen Jesus will reward His bride with 'an inheritance incorruptible and undefiled and that does not fade away, reserved in heaven'. This reward has reference to saving grace freely given but also extra persevering grace promised in the Covenant of Redemption, 'who are kept by the power of God through faith for salvation ready to be revealed in the last time'. The end of planet earth as we know it will usher in the new heavens and new earth (Rev. 22; cf. Isa. 65 and 66).

Between the new birth and death lies ordained suffering in our fallen world so Christians are to hope to the end when tested using faith as an anchor for the soul (Heb. 6:19). However, hope will no longer be required when we are raised to be like Him. Peter insists that this glorious prospect of salvation and promised hope should elicit joy beyond all normal levels:

- 'Whom having not seen you love. Though now you do not see Him, yet believing, you rejoice with joy inexpressible and full of glory, receiving the end of your faith-the salvation of *your* souls' (1 Pet. 1:8–9).

Let our love for Jesus encourage joy and perseverance. It is God's mercy that is the source of redemption's plan. So instead of doubting Jesus we are to bless God for Him and for the hope of resurrection to come. We have been delivered from sin *and* death now our hearts go out to Him as we rejoice and know the Spirit's peace.

The 'Amen' presents himself to the Laodiceans (church) with all its problems and failures because He is, 'the Faithful and True Witness'. Therefore He speaks the truth to them through their 'angel' (Rev. 3:14) and speaks the truth with love (Rev. 3:19a). Because He is the *Amen* He guarantees and fulfils the promises of God, i.e.:

- He completes what is necessary to gain our full salvation being the: *True One.*
- He supplies essential grace to persevere in the Christian life being the: *Faithful One.*
- He fulfils all the promises of the gospel being the: *First and the Last.*

Our reaction

How should one react to these things? Firstly, the resurrection is to be believed as true and trusted as being faithful to the historical facts. In the light of the Scriptures, Christians can be confident that the gospel is able to save them and present them blameless before the throne of God believing that because Jesus Christ lives they shall live also. Secondly, the resurrection is to be 'gossiped' to others with the hope that they believe and are saved. Not only this, but people should be told that the risen Jesus, at His Second Advent, shall descend from heaven on the Judgement Day with a shout when the last trumpet of God sounds to establish His kingdom on earth. This will change everything and everyone in a 'moment in the twinkling of an eye' (1 Cor. 15:51–53). Thirdly, believers are to honour Christ who atoned for sins and conquered death by living in the power of their risen Lord full of hope and joy in the Holy Spirit and participate committedly and regularly to weekly public worship. Fourthly, wait with patience while facing the future with hope and the assurance of faith, which anticipates the promised inheritance that nothing can spoil nor diminish. Charles Spurgeon is pertinent here:

Child of God, death hath lost its sting, because the devil's power over it is destroyed. Then cease to fear dying. Ask grace from God the Holy Ghost, that by an intimate knowledge and a firm belief of your Redeemer's death, you may be strengthened for that dread hour. Living near the cross of Calvary you may think of death with pleasure, and welcome it when it comes with intense delight. It is sweet to die in the Lord: it is a covenant-blessing to sleep in Jesus. Death is no longer banishment, it is a return from exile, a going home to the many mansions where the loved ones already dwell. The distance between glorified spirits in heaven and militant saints on earth seems great; but it is not so. Listen to the answer, 'Absent from the body, present with the Lord.' Then, O child of God, what is there for you to fear in death, seeing that through the death of your Lord its curse and sting are destroyed? And now it is but a Jacob's ladder whose foot is in the dark grave, but its top reaches to glory everlasting.[13]

Saviour, come! We long to see Thee,
Long to dwell with thee above;
And to know in full communion,
All the sweetness of Thy love,
   Come, Lord Jesus!
   Come, Lord Jesus!
Take Thy waiting people home.
         (William Williams)

NOTES

1 Westminster Confession of Faith 32; 3 and Baptist Confession of Faith 1689, 31; 3.

2 Quoted from, Sergent, *Gems*, p. 253.

3 S B Ferguson, 'The Reformed Doctrine of Sonship', *Pulpit and People, Essays in honour of William Still*, Edinburgh, 1986), p. 87.

4 *Reformed Book of Common Order*, 1988.

5 Heaven is a place. In Scripture it is spoken of as a country and a city (Luke 20:35; Heb. 11:10, 16). It is the Father's house where the holy angels dwell with Him (John 14:1; Isa 6; Rev. 5).

6 In this way, heaven is open to humankind made fit for heaven by the atoning blood of the Lamb of God. This is the preparation He speaks about in John 14.

7 See, Luke 23: 43; 2 Cor. 12: 2–3.

8 Although the Bible explicitly speaks of Christ's appearance a second time, the phrase Second Coming occurs nowhere in the New Testament. Many passages, however, speak of His return. In the New Testament it is referred to over 300 times.

9 Nelson, CD_ROM, *Believers Bible Commentary*.

10 Calvin commenting on 1 Cor. 6:14 ('God both raised up the Lord and will also raise us up by His power') says, 'we will be sharers in blessed immortality and heavenly glory along with Christ. There is a similar thought in Colossians 3:1; "If then ye were raised together with Christ" etc. There is this difference, however, that here He is speaking about the final resurrection only, while in that passage He also speaks of the first resurrection, in other words, of the grace of the Holy Spirit, by which we are transformed into a new life' (see, John Calvin, *New Testament Commentaries: 1 Corinthians* (Grand Rapids, MI: William B Eerdmans Publishing, 1996), p. 129).

11 F F Bruce, *The Epistle to the Colossians, To Philemon, and To the Ephesians* (Grand Rapids, MI: Eerdmans Publishing, 1984), p. 55, n. 73.

12 Nelson CD_ROM; (Hebrew: {אָמֵן}, Modern, *amen*; Greek: ἀμήν; Arabic: آمِين).

13 Spurgeon, *Morning & Evening* (20 April) [adapted].

Resurrection, the cults and soul-sleep

Do not weep, she is not dead but sleeping. (Luke 8:52)

The annihilationists have only a comparatively small following because there is a consciousness in all men that death does not end all. The idea of immortality is so deeply rooted in the human mind that most unrepentant persons are afraid to die because they are worried, sometimes terrified, by the uncertainty of what lies beyond.[1]

V arious resurrection heresies have existed since apostolic times in one form or another.[2] Gnosticism blended Eastern mysticism with Greek dualism claiming that matter is completely evil.[3] Rejection of bodily resurrection was present in some churches during the latter years of the first century. An example of which was Paul's warning to Timothy about Hymenaeus and Philetus for they 'have strayed concerning the truth, saying that the resurrection is already past; and they overthrow the faith of some' (2 Tim. 2:17–18).

The Cults

The major 'Christian' cults are well known but sit outside conservative Protestant denominations.[4] They themselves are generally happy about this not wanting to be linked with evangelical reformed ecclesiology or soteriology and they are particularly scathing regarding Roman Catholicism and its clergy. It is true however, that the Mormons and the Seventh Day Adventists and others would like to be regarded as part of Christendom as their eschatology is derived from the Adventist movements in the eighteenth and early nineteenth centuries in USA.

Christian Science teaches that Jesus did not atone for sin on the cross but was merely an example of the kind of life we should live. They believe He did not rise from the dead nor ascend into heaven and they teach the resurrection is a 'Spiritualizing of thought, a new and higher idea of immortality, or spiritual existence.' The *Seventh Day Adventist* (SDAs) view of the resurrection is contaminated by their doctrine of man and their denial that the soul survives death (this they have in common with the Jehovah's Witnesses). Article 10, of their *Fundamental Beliefs*, says 'That condition of man in death is one of unconsciousness. That all men, good and evil alike, remain in the grave from death to the resurrection', and that 'sleep' is unconsciousness broken at the 'awakening at the resurrection'.[5] They teach that there will be resurrection for all men. A A Hoekema is sure, however, that 'the Adventists teach *soul-extinction*' and 'conditional immortality'. The SDAs believe in three resurrections.[6] Unbelievers will be raised from the dead after the millennium, but they will be raised only to be annihilated and believers *before* the resurrection to reign with Christ. There is a 'special resurrection' before the Second Coming so that those who are guilty of the trial and crucifixion of Jesus can be judged and those who were faithful unto death by keeping the seventh-day Sabbath will see His return. All those still alive will ascend to heaven for the millennium to decide how much punishment unbelievers will experience before annihilation. *Christadelphians* believe that the Son came into existence only when born. Before that He 'existed potentially in the divine will'. After Jesus's resurrection His humanity (they say) was transferred into divinity. They believe that, after death, they are in a state of non-existence, knowing nothing until the resurrection at the return of Christ. Following the Judgement 'the accepted' receive the gift of immortality, and live with Christ on a restored earth, assisting Jesus to establish the Kingdom of God and to rule over the mortal population for a thousand years (the Millennium). The kingdom will be centred upon Israel, but Jesus Christ will also reign over all the other nations on the earth. Some unorthodox Christadelphians believe that the kingdom itself is not worldwide but limited to the land of Israel promised to Abraham and ruled over in the past by David, with a worldwide empire.[7] The *Jehovah's Witnesses* say that there is no soul which survives after death and at death nothing survives and man becomes completely non-existent. Their view is one of soul-extinction.[8] However, their doctrine exempts their 144,000 elect members who at death, 'do not sink into nonexistence, but are immediately changed into immortal spirits'.[9]

Way of salvation

The cults' way of salvation subtly sets aside the doctrine of justification by grace alone through faith alone found in the New Testament and replaces it with a charter of works. They believe salvation is the reward for keeping the commandments of God and doing good works as defined by them. In this they fail to understand that salvation is by grace alone, through faith alone in (the biblical) Christ alone grasping the full implication that, 'if by grace it is no longer of works' (Rom. 11:6). The doctrine of justification was central to the Protestant Reformation and states that salvation does not depend on human acts of love or kindness but it is the free gift of God given to all who believe the gospel (Eph. 2:8–9; Rom. 4:2–5; Acts 16:31; Titus 3:5; Gal. 3:26; 1 Peter 1:23). Each cult regards itself as the chosen people of God on earth. It is convinced it alone is the only true and faithful community of God's people. The cults, however, have no appreciation of the biblical doctrine of 'one holy catholic church' (i.e. the universal church) composed of the true people in all ages and from all nations (John 17:20–21; Eph. 4:3–7; 1 Cor. 12:1; John 2:1–2; Rev. 7:9; Eph. 5:25–27). Resurrection for the cults is dependent on obedience to the rule of *their* community.

Soul-sleep

The soul's immortal existence is denied by most cults and is similar in thinking to the ancient [Greek] Epicureans, 'As long as we are alive, *death does not exist for us, and when death appears, we* no longer exist'.[10] However, William Henry Green in his monologue, 'The Doctrine of Immortality in the Old Testament' says that, 'from the very beginning of the old economy the immortality of the soul and a future state of unending existence were revealed and were believed.' The Scriptures speak, 'of man's creation, who alone of all terrestrial beings was made in God's image (Gen. 1:27) and whose soul, breathed into Him by the Lord, is expressly distinct from His material body (Gen. 2:7; Ecc. 12:7).' He also notes that the translations of Enoch (Gen. 5:24) and Elijah (2 Kgs 2:1) recognised this reality (cf. 1 Sam. 28:14; Isa. 14:9–27). Here we see a continued, conscious, and intelligent existence after death. 'An immortality without God is devoid of all reality or significance, and falls to the level of the pagan notion, which is as far as possible from all that is taught us in the Word of God.'[11] Hoekema is helpful here also: the soul is not inherently indestructible as Greek philosophy would argue. The Bible teaches no such view of the soul. We are dependent on God for our existence and eternal life as it is only found in fellowship with God in Christ (Acts 17:28; Phil. 2:21–23). Those out of fellowship will continue to exist after death but not in happiness or peace (Luke 16:23–25; 2 Peter 2:9), for 'what profit is it to a man if He gains the whole world, and loses His own soul?' (Matt. 16:26).[12] Unlike the soul, which is alive both physically and eternally, the spirit can be either alive, as in the case of believers (1 Pet. 3:18), or dead as unbelievers are (Col. 2:13; Eph. 2:4–5).

Modernity

The modern cults oppose the doctrine of the intermediate state, teaching rather that the concept of soul-sleep is taught in the Bible. However, Jesus's words to Jairus ('a ruler of the synagogue'), 'Do not weep, she is not dead but sleeping' (Luke 8:52) make it plain, teaching that children and believing loved ones, who have crossed over the river of death before us, are safe in the arms of Jesus and safe on His gentle breast. Their bodies are at rest (asleep) and their souls are alive in heaven where they await the resurrection *shout* which will summon all the redeemed (John 5:28–29; Thess. 4:16; Rev. 20:4). Some argue that, 'sleep' corresponds to soul-sleep, i.e. a state of non-existence as did the Epicureans and Sadducees of old. However, 'sleep' is often a euphemism for death in the New Testament (John 11:11–12; Acts 7:60; 1 Thess. 5:10). Soul-sleep is clearly refuted in different portions of Scripture. In 1 Thessalonians it reads, 'even so God will bring with Him those who sleep in Jesus's (1 Thess. 4:14). Obviously '*those*' refer not to soul-sleeping persons but to those alive in heaven that are destined to return with Christ Jesus when He comes a second time (1 Thess. 3:13). Stephen, the first Christian martyr asked, 'Lord Jesus receive my spirit' as He was about to die (Acts 7:59), believing that death took Him into the presence of God. Richard Baxter comments on Stephen's words, 'If the Lord received it, it is neither asleep, nor dead nor annihilated; but it is where He is, and beholds His glory.'[13]

Synoptic gospels and the first resurrection

The concept of soul-sleep was one on which Christ and the religious Sadducees clashed in the Gospel of Mark (12:18–27). This Jewish sect did not believe in life after death in any form. They did not believe in the resurrection of the dead and in one incident where Jesus clashed with them they approached Jesus with a 'what if' question designed to test His understanding of the afterlife (cf. Matt. 22:33; Luke 20:27–40). 'Suppose', they asked, 'a woman had seven husbands in this life, and each of them died without leaving children whose wife would she be in the age to come?' Answering, firstly, Jesus said that they were wrong to suggest that earthly relationships, such as marriage, will continue after the resurrection, 'when they rise from the dead, they neither marry nor are given in marriage, but are like angels of God in heaven' (v. 25). Secondly, He pointed out that they were wrong in not believing in the resurrection, 'concerning the dead that they rise, have you not read in the book of Moses, in the *burning* bush *passage*, how God spoke to Him, saying, *I am the God of Abraham, the God of Isaac, and the God of Jacob?*' (v. 26). Jesus conveyed the clear thought that the souls of Abraham, Isaac and Jacob are very much alive but their bodies are 'asleep' (cf. Ps. 73:24). Jesus's two-part answer showed them the power of God, 'He is not the God of the dead but the God of the living. You are therefore greatly mistaken' (v. 27). When it comes to the Judgement Day their souls are not re-created because they are (already) with God and wait the resurrection and new heavens and earth (1 Thess. 3:13, 4:14; Rev. 20:11–21:1). In Luke's account of this confrontation with the scholars we find added content. When Jesus was asked about the resurrection He speaks of the dead, who are worthy of resurrection and who cannot 'die anymore, for they are equal to the angels and are sons of God, being sons of the resurrection' (Luke 20:36). These 'sons of the resurrection' are the children of God through faith in Jesus Christ and are promised to be like Him (the *first* resurrection is spoken of in Rev. 20:4–6). Therefore, the redemption day includes soul and body being indwelt by the Spirit of God. As Hendriksen says, 'apart from Christianity there was no solid basis for hope in connection with the after-life'.[14]

Soul and Spirit

The term soul (Gk. *psuchee*) refers to the inner life of a person, the seat of emotions, and the centre of human personality (Gen. 2:7), it engages our emotions (Ps. 86:4), knowing (Ps. 139:14), and remembrance (Lam. 3:20). This means as human being they remained distinct from all other (Heb. *nephesh*) life. In the New Testament, Jesus spoke of His soul as being exceedingly sorrowful (Matt. 26:28). Mary, the mother of Jesus, proclaimed that her soul magnifies the Lord (Luke 1:46). John prayed that Gaius would prosper in all things and be in health, just as 'your soul prospers' (3 John 1:2).[15] In Ecclesiastes, the man (person) is differentiated from His soul. The context is the preacher stating that God-ordained pleasures are found in the common things of life like eating and drinking as the result of honest work:

Nothing *is* better for a man *than* that He should eat and drink, and *that* His soul should enjoy good in His labour. This also, I saw, was from the hand of God. (Ecc. 2:24)[16]

The soul is that which makes a human body alive. Jesus, like King Solomon, differentiates *the man* from *His soul*: 'For what will it profit a man if He gains the whole world, and loses His own soul?' (Mark 8:36–37). This is also implied in the reviving ministry of the prophet Elijah. He saw a child brought back to life by stretching himself upon the child three times and praying that God would let the child's soul come back into Him (1 Kgs. 17:21). The Apostle Paul confirmed Solomon's outlook. He said that if there is no resurrection of the dead then the best policy is, 'Let us eat and drink, for tomorrow we die!' (1 Cor. 15:32).[17]

Whenever the word 'soul' is used, it can refer to the whole person, whether physically alive or in the afterlife. The word 'spirit' both in Hebrew and Greek has the concept of *breath* or *wind* at their roots. We understand the diversity of uses between the two words by looking at their context. The spiritual part of believers in Jesus Christ is that which responds to the things that come from the Spirit of God, understanding and discerning them spiritually. The lost souls who are spiritually dead perceive the things of the Spirit to be 'foolishness' because, in their spiritually dead conditions, their ability to discern the things of the Spirit is lacking (1 Cor. 2:12–14). The spirit is that part of us that is enabled by God to know and worship Him, the part of humanity that 'connects' with God, who himself is Spirit (John 4:24). While the two words are often used interchangeably, the primary distinction between soul and spirit in man is that the soul is the animate life, or the seat of the senses, desires, affections and appetites, but the spirit is that part of us that connects, or refuses to connect, to God. Our spirits relate to His Spirit, either accepting His promptings and conviction, thereby proving that we belong to Him (Rom. 8:16) or resisting Him and proving that we do not have spiritual life (Acts 7:51).[18]

New Testament Proof

- Can we find more proof from the sacred text of Scripture on life after death?
- Paul's account of His experience of 'Paradise', which He equates with the *third heaven* (2 Cor. 12:1–6) and the dwelling place of God, confirms that the Bible reveals only three heavens; these are the atmospheric heavens, the stellar heavens and the *third heaven*. (The concept of a 'seven heavens' is not a Judeo-Christian concept but that of Islam.)[19]
- The story of the rich man and Lazarus (Luke 16) shows us that the dead are in a state of consciousness after death and either in heaven or hell. This story, which is much more than a parable gives us insight into the afterlife.
- In the story of the thief on the cross (Luke 23) we hear Jesus telling the repentant thief that his soul will be transported to heaven: 'today you will be with me in Paradise' (v. 43). Loraine Boettner in his book *Immortality* says regarding this, 'these words would have afforded little comfort if he were to sink into a state of dead unconsciousness only to be awakened by the judgement trumpet.'[20]
- Revelation 6:9–10 refers to those souls who still exist after death and are conscious and so, 'souls here cannot simply mean living creatures or persons, for it makes no sense to say, "The people of those who had been slain" or "the living creatures of those who had been slain."'[21]
- Revelation 7:9–17 records a vision where John sees believers in heaven (the intermediate state); they are not asleep but are rather

serving God 'day and night' (v. 15). These blessed ones are not in the memory of God, nor are they impassive or in an unconscious state, but rather they are active in the service of their Saviour. This, of course, is what they always wanted—to serve God perfectly, totally and unequivocally. This will be heaven indeed!

- In John 11:11–14 we read of the resurrection of Lazarus, the friend of Jesus. He died while Jesus was out of town but Jesus said of Him, 'Lazarus is *fallen asleep*.' In 1 Thessalonians, Paul speaks of those who have fallen asleep, 'I do not want you to be ignorant, brethren, concerning those who have *fallen asleep*, lest you sorrow as others who have no hope' (4:13). Therefore, we can see that the New Testament talks of dying (metaphorically) as sleep which promise instant hope of heaven (2 Cor. 5:8).

- Luke's Gospel tells the story of the death of a twelve-year-old girl and the subsequent miracle by Jesus of her *resurrection* (8:40–42, 49–56). there we are told in the narrative that the child's father—a ruler of the synagogue—was given the sad news of her death moments after He met with Jesus to request that He visit his very sick child for healing (v. 42). However, before this could happen a messenger tells the father, 'your daughter is dead. Do not trouble the teacher' (v. 49). What pain and overwhelming sorrow must have gripped this parent's heart at that moment. Any hope of recovery was now gone and temporary darkness descended over His heart. It was the voice of the Saviour who restored hope to the bereaved father saying, 'do not be afraid; only believe, and she will be made well' (v. 50). The presence of Christ meant that the power of God was among them. When this story is read, the question is often asked, 'Was the girl really dead?' It is clear that she was not in a coma (although this condition would have vanished at Jesus's command) because the family friends and mourners were convinced that she most certainly *was* dead and they laughed scornfully at any thought to the contrary (v. 53). She was dead; but her spirit had left her body and 'returned to God who gave it' (Ecc. 12:7). Death is sleep for the body while the soul waits in heaven for the resurrection day (1 Cor. 15:54–55; 1 Thess. 4:13–18).

For Charles Spurgeon, death is sleep in Jesus:

Let us not imagine that *the soul* sleeps in insensibility. 'Today shalt thou be with me in paradise,' is the whisper of Christ to every dying saint. They 'sleep in Jesus,' but their souls are before the throne of God, praising him day and night in his temple, singing hallelujahs to him who washed them from their sins in his blood. The idea connected with sleep is '*rest*,' and that is the thought which the Spirit of God would convey to us. They went to their rest but they wake up in beauty and glory. Blessed is death, since it, through the divine power, disrobes us of this work-day garment, to clothe us with the wedding garment of incorruption. Blessed are those who 'sleep in Jesus'.[22]

The historic miracle of 'resurrection' in Luke 8 was a type of the glorious resurrection to come.

My hope is built on nothing less
than Jesus's blood and righteousness;
I dare not trust the sweetest frame,
but wholly lean on Jesus's name.

On Christ the solid rock I stand
All other ground is sinking sand.
   (Edward Mote, 1797–1874)

NOTES

1 Boettner, *Immortality*, p. 122.

2 A recent book by B D Ehrman, *When Christians Gave us Hell: A History of the After Life*

(Oneworld, 2020) does not take the resurrection seriously nor the inspiration of the Word of God and doubts its veracity, authority and sufficiency!

3 Gnosticism sets itself against true Christianity at every point. It described God calling Him the Demiurge. This false teaching was faced by the church in the second and third centuries AD. But far from being ancient history, Gnostic beliefs are rife today. Of course, not many people call themselves Gnostics. But their approach to issues such as transsexualism is clearly rooted in Gnostic thought. Understanding Gnosticism and the Christian response to it will encourage and equip believers to stand firm. Gnosticism was successfully rejected by the early church but never quite went away. It has enjoyed a revival in today's popular culture, not least in New Age thinking. The Englishman and Beatles guitarist John Lennon said, 'The only true Christians were the Gnostics, who believe in self-knowledge, i.e. becoming Christ themselves, reaching the Christ within.' https://www.christian.org.uk/wp-content/uploads/gnosticism.pdf

4 See my book, "Engaging with Islam". Chapter 14, *Cults and new religions*, pp. 153–155 for a definition.

5 Help is acknowledged from A A Hoekema, *The Four Cults* (Exeter: The Paternoster Press, 1969), p. 135.

6 However, because the SDA's don't believe in an immortal soul their resurrection is better understood as a new creation.

7 https://en.wikipedia.org/wiki/John_Thomas_(Christadelphian)

8 Hoekema, *The Four Cults*, p. 345.

9 Ibid. p. 348. This happened in 1918 and that number is now complete and no more can be added to it.

10 W Hendriksen, *1 Thessalonian Commentary*, p. 111.

11 W H Green, *Conflict and Triumph* (Edinburgh: Banner of Truth Trust, 1999), pp. 173–4, 176.

12 See AA Hoekema, *The Bible and the Future*, p. 90.

13 R Baxter, *The Saints' Everlasting Rest* (London: E Grant Richards, 1907), p. 185

14 W Hendriksen, *1 & 2 Thessalonians*, p. 111.

15 CD-ROM, 'SOUL' adapted.

16 15 English versions translate *nephesh* as 'soul'; https://biblehub.com/ecclesiastes/2–24.htm

17 The Hebrew word *nephesh* in almost every passage of the Old Testament is answered by *psuche* in Greek with *psuchee*. It is the animating principle of the body and represents the life of man. It also included bodily appetites and desires. *Nephesh* is also rendered mind and heart in the sense of desire and inclination. See, R B Girdlestone, (Grand Rapids, MI: W B Eerdmans Publishing, 1978), p. 55ff.

18 Help found from https://www.researchgate.net/post/What_is_the_difference_between_

soul_and_spirit2#:~:text=While%20the%20two%20words%20are,refuses%20to%20 connect%2C%20to%20God.

19 The New Testament speaks only of three heavens (2 Cor. 12) while the Quran speaks of seven (Suras 2:29; 41:12; 65:12; 71:15).

20 Boettner, *Immortality*, p. 113.

21 Hoekema, *The Four Cults*, p. 348.

22 C H Spurgeon, *Morning & Evening* (29 June), (McLean, VI: MacDonald Publishing Co., no date), adapted.

Appendix 2

Resurrection and Islam

The holy angels came and took Jesus out by the window that looketh toward the south. They bare Him and placed Him in the third heaven ... Judas was so changed in speech and in face to be like Jesus that we believed Him to be Jesus. (*Gospel of Barnabas*)

I slam would discredit *His-story* by casting doubt on the validity of the four Gospels and their reports of the resurrection. The resurrection of Jesus is not regarded as true by Muslims as the Quran claims that Jesus did not die on the cross; rather, the planned death of Jesus was thwarted when another person was crucified in His place: 'They did not kill Him, nor did they crucify Him, but it only seemed to them [as if it had been so]' (Sura 4:157). Muslims are therefore taught, in accordance with this Sura, that whoever died on the cross (if it actually happened), it was *not* Jesus Christ: 'a substitute was made to look like Jesus and was crucified in His place while Jesus was taken straight up to heaven (without dying)'.[1] These ideas have no historical substance or theological credibility. No secular historian doubts that Jesus was a historical person and that He was crucified and buried. So this assertion that Jesus did not die on the cross is without historical foundation.

It is believed among Muslims that there was no atonement made by the death of Jesus of Nazareth or any other 'Jesus'. Rather, the planned death of Jesus was thwarted when another person was crucified in the real Jesus's place, that man was Judas. Muslims are therefore taught that whoever died on the cross (if it actually happened) was *not* Jesus. This is established by the quote above from Sura 4. Muslim belief is based on the authority of the *Gospel of Barnabas* written by someone claiming to be one of the twelve disciples of Jesus, 'not earlier than the fourteenth century, i.e. well over a thousand years after Christ and 700 years after

Muhammad'. It is asserted that it was Judas Iscariot who was crucified while Jesus was snatched away to the third heaven.[2] Because Islam believes that there was no death of Jesus at Calvary but transference into the 'third' heaven therefore there can be no resurrection of Jesus for the dead in Islamic theology.

The New Testament begs to differ. The Apostle Peter not only spoke about Jesus Christ's resurrection and its implication at Pentecost in Acts 2 but also to the 'Rulers of the people and the elders of Israel', in Acts 4:

> Then Peter, filled with the Holy Spirit, said to them, '… let it be known to you all, and to all the people of Israel, that by the name of Jesus Christ of Nazareth, whom you crucified, whom God raised from the dead … This is the *stone which was rejected by you builders, which has become the chief cornerstone*. Nor is there salvation in any other, for there is no other name under heaven given among men by which we must be saved.' (vv. 8a, 10–12)

This denial of the death and third day resurrection of Jesus by Islam strikes at the very heart of the gospel and is aimed at the foundation of the church. This makes the two religions incompatible.

The sign of Jonah[3]

Christians must oppose all attempts to deny, invalidate or rewrite the resurrection accounts as found in the Gospels. Such attempts are on the increase, with more and more literature being produced from Islamic sources to discredit the historical accounts of the four Gospels. One such effort is centred on the New Testament phrase 'the sign of the prophet Jonah'. The phrase is found in Matthew 12:40 and Luke 11:29 (cf. John 2:19) where it was used by our Lord during His teaching ministry with the apostles. In His account, Matthew makes it clear that the sign of Jonah was the resurrection of Christ from the dead: He said:

> An evil and adulterous generation seeks after a sign, and no sign will be given to it except the sign

of the prophet Jonah. For as Jonah was three days and three nights in the belly of the great fish, so will the Son of Man be three days and three nights in the heart of the earth. (Matt. 12:39–40)

Just as Jonah spent three days and three nights in the belly of the great fish, so Christ would be three days and three nights in the tomb and on the third day He would rise from the dead. The resurrection is a sign to the world that Jesus Christ is the Son of God and the sign of Jonah was Christ's resurrection on the first day of the week. This therefore means that the sign of the new covenant is remembrance of the resurrection of Jesus Christ on the Lord's-Day (Rev. 1:10).

The Gospels signify the importance of the plan of redemption and the content of the gospel message. It lays emphasis on the time when Christ was in the tomb before He rose bodily at His resurrection, and on the resurrection as a sign that tells the world that Jesus Christ is Lord. Islam refuses to accept that Jesus was in the tomb for three days and nights and endeavours to interpret the Bible in a way that contradicts the New Testament's testimony. 'One Islamic writer enquires, 'A fish swallows Jonah. Was he dead or alive when swallowed? Surely dead men don't cry and don't pray! Was he dead or alive for three days and nights? Alive! Alive! Alive! Is the unanimous answer from the Jew, the Christian and the Muslim! If Jonah was alive for three days and three nights, then Jesus also ought to have been. Jesus is *supposed* to be in the tomb on the night of Friday … You will no doubt note that the *grand total* is *one* day and *two* nights, and not three days and three nights. Is this not the mightiest hoax in history?'[4] Muslims differed as to how long he spent in the belly of the fish. Some said three days; this was the view of Qatadah.[5]

The Christian faith is rooted in historical fact and not fiction. The Bible proclaims the fact but does not attempt to describe the process of Christ's resurrection. Because of the words 'I am the resurrection and the life' (John 11:25) those who trust in Jesus Christ will share in His everlasting victory. As A W Pink puts it:

Then shall be fulfilled that mystical word, 'I say to you that many will come from east and west, and sit down with Abraham, Isaac, and Jacob in the kingdom of heaven' (Matt. 8:11). As the Lord Jesus declared, 'I lay down My life for the sheep. And other sheep I have which are not of this fold; them also I must bring, and they will hear My voice; and there will be one flock *and* one shepherd' (John 10:15, 16). Then it shall be that Christ will 'gather *together in one* the children of God who were scattered abroad' (John 11:52)—not only among all nations, but through all dispensations.[6]

The Easter story[7]

The Easter story is the story of God's love for this fallen world and the resurrection is the triumph of Jesus Christ over the last enemy which is death. This is why the Easter message is about life and not death. Because of this, those who trust in Him and believe the gospel can be confident they will share in the resurrection to come on the last day. When the resurrection day arrives, believers will be given a body like the risen Saviour's; it shall be perfect, fitted for a spiritual existence and it will have the power of an endless life (1 Cor. 15:44). Believing in Jesus who, 'was raised again for our justification' (Rom. 4:25, AV) and His words that He is, 'the resurrection and the life' justifies sinners, saving them from hell. There could have been no justification if Christ had remained in the tomb. However, the fact that He rose tells us that the work of atonement is finished, the price has been paid, and God is infinitely satisfied with the sin-atoning work of the Saviour.

NOTES

1 Patrick Sookhdeo, *Is the Muslim Isa the Biblical Jesus?* (McLean, VA: Isaac Publishing, 2012), p. 8.

2 Ibid. pp. 27–28. *The Gospel of Barnabas*, ed. Aisha Bawany (Karachi: Ashram Publications, 1976), quoted in Peter G Riddell and Peter Cotterell, *Islam in Conflict: Past, Present and Future* (Leicester: IVP, 2003), pp. 78–79. The Ahmadis teach that Jesus was crucified and was taken down alive and resuscitated in the cold tomb with the help of Nicodemus. He subsequently went east and died and was buried in Kashmir (ibid. pp. 79–80). John

Gilchrist concludes, 'No one knows who actually wrote the *Gospel of Barnabas* but what is known, without a shadow of a doubt, is that whoever it was, it was certainly not the Apostle Barnabas. It was probably a Muslim in Spain who, being the victim of the reconquest of His country, decided to take private revenge by composing a false gospel under the assumed name of Barnabas.' *Origins and Sources of the Gospel of Barnabas* (Sheffield: Fellowship of Faith for the Muslims, 1992), p. 29.

3 See also Chapter 8 in my book *The Real Lord's Prayer* (Leominster: Day One, 2012).

4 Ahmed Deedat, 'What Was the Sign of Jonah?' at www.islamworld.net/jonah.html; accessed March 2012.

5 The name of a companion of Mohammed.

6 Pink, *An Exposition of Hebrews*, p. 891.

7 Easter is not a biblical word. It is used in the Germanic languages and is of pagan origin. It is linked with the festival of the spring vernal equinox when the sun crosses the equator, making day in length to night. However, it coincides with the time of the Jewish Passover. Both William Tyndale and Miles Coverdale used 'Easter' in their English New Testaments because they rendered the Greek word *pascha* (pasca) that way. Today however, most modern versions translate it as 'Passover' (Acts 12:4).

Matthew 27:45, 52–53

'The tombs were opened. This shows that the death of the Saviour had—and is still having—significance for the entire universe. (William Hendriksen)

The synoptic Gospel chronicles are aware of the historic bodily resurrection of Jesus Christ from the dead on the third day (this we have discussed above) and they—with some surprise for first-time readers—note jointly the supernatural events which coincided with Jesus's death and resurrection. These were (beginning from the sixth hour—noon—on the day of Jesus's crucifixion):

• When Jesus died nature mourned.
• When Jesus died Gentiles were grafted in.
• When Jesus died resurrection was promised.
• When Jesus died resurrection was sealed.

The miracles of Calvary were a chain of events which served as signs to the Jews, Sadducees, Pharisees and, indeed the whole populous of Jerusalem (and not only the apostles and the followers of Jesus of Nazareth) that He was someone very special. At that moment God was marking His death with signs and wonders both in nature and by miracles. These point to the greatness of Jesus Christ in direct and close connection with His Messianic mission and clearly reflect the importance of His death and coming resurrection. The mysterious events are from heaven and they are a 'class of wonders by themselves'.[1] Their historic purpose was to bring attention to the inhabitants of Jerusalem that Jesus from Nazareth is Christ of Scripture: the promised suffering Servant of Jehovah (Isa. 53). What a surprise and shock this must have been to the Sadducees and enemies of Jesus to think that dead and buried bodies were raised in contradiction to their belief systems while demonstration that the One they were happy to see crucified was who He claimed to be

(John 6:35; 10:7; 11:25). These events are given space in the synoptic narratives (Matt 27:39–49; Mark 15:33–38; Luke 23:44–45a) and linked closely with the last and seventh cry of the Saviour when on the cross.

1. When Jesus died nature mourned (v. 45)

Jesus, when on the cross and nearing His last breath, there darkness covered the land which lasted from the sixth hour until the ninth hour (12 pm to 3 pm):

Now from the sixth hour until the ninth hour there was darkness over all the land. And about the ninth hour Jesus cried out with a loud voice, saying, 'Eli, Eli, lama sabachthani?' that is, 'My God, My God, why have You forsaken Me?' (vv. 45–46)

This occurred when the sun was at its zenith and should have been blazing. It was as Charles Spurgeon noted, 'midnight at midday'.[2] This darkness was unexpected and its effect induced fear, and shock. This was not the first time nature witnessed to the Christ greatness and glory: the star in the East that the Magi saw shine brightly at Jesus birth was a supernatural event and we are told also to expect nature to rejoice at the coming King for heaven:

Immediately after the tribulation of those days the sun will be darkened, and the moon will not give its light; the stars will fall from heaven, and the powers of the heavens will be shaken. Then the sign of the Son of Man will appear in heaven. (Matt. 24:29–30)

So it was at the cross; when nature mourned for its Creator by throwing a veil over Jesus sufferings as He became sin for us, thus hiding His terrible pains and intense agony of soul. The three hours of darkness gives meaning to the cry of anguish heard from the lips of the dying Saviour: 'God wrapped His Lamb in darkness to hide Him from human eyes', an anonymous speaker once said, symbolising the inconceivable sufferings of Christ in His death (v. 46).

To most people there [that day] it was simply a village carpenter, a wandering preacher in pain, but in the plan and sober purpose of Almighty God, "He became sin for us, who knew no sin, that we might be made the righteousness of God in Him" (2 Cor. 5:21). He died at the time of the evening sacrifice and stood in our place becoming the atoning Lamb and sin bearer for our redemption. The judgement of God on Jesus was a legal verdict and a payment for sin's transgression fulfilling the justice of God. God passed judgment on our sins not His, when He was 'made sin for us'. There was no escape for Jesus for He came to save us. The darkness points to the work of vicarious atonement, i.e. God's reconciling work through His Son in order to undo the consequences of the Fall into sin, bringing death.

2. When Jesus died the Gentiles were grafted in (v. 51a)

The scope of His death is announced in the temple and the priests of God saw God's hand at work and therefore God's will if they understood the event before them, viz. the Gentiles are now accepted into the true Vine, 'Then, behold, the veil of the temple was torn in two from top to bottom.' The tearing of the temple curtain followed the sixth and seventh cries of the crucified One. It was not the result of the earth shaking which split rocks. If it had come as a consequence of the earthquake why did it not shake to pieces the building also where it hung? The rendering of the curtain was quite independent of the quake and was the effect of the death cry of the Saviour as He expired His last breath (Luke 23:46; John 19:30). It was at 3 pm, the time of the evening sacrifice. The temple priests would have been in front of the veil and engaged in their preparations. So without warning, at the moment the Son died, the great veil was ripped in two from the top to the bottom. What a surprise and what a symbol! The curtain separated the two sanctuaries; the inner (holy of holies) from the outer (the holy place). This separation was not violated before, not for 1,500 years! The outer sanctuary was for the preparation of sacrifices while the inner was only for the High Priest once a year on the Day of Atonement (Yom Kippur) for presentation of the atoning offering.

God meant Jesus's death to be noticed, deeply considered and the event confirmed by reliable witnesses. He wanted it known that the door of salvation was now open to the Gentile nations because His Son is the Saviour of the world (John 3:16). If the Gospel record is false it would have been so easy to speak against it and the expose it as a lie. However, this being the truth the priests who witnessed the event would have reported it with awe and wonder. No wonder we read (later), 'a great many of the priests were obedient to the faith' (Acts 6:7).

The epistle to the Hebrews tells us that the curtain is a type of Christ: the veil made for linen represents His human nature and the rods and hooks of gold His divinity, while the 'cunning work' (i.e. skilled work) Jesus Christ's incarnation life as the God-man:

Therefore, brethren, having boldness to enter the Holiest by the blood of Jesus, by a new and living way which He consecrated for us, through the veil, that is, His flesh. (Heb. 10:19–20)

3. When Jesus died resurrection was promised

The earthquake was linked to the preceding miracles that day following on from Jesus penultimate cry when He cried out with a loud voice, and yielded up His spirit. (v. 50) saying, 'Father, *into Your hands I commit My spirit*' so, '*having said this, He breathed His last*' (Luke 23:46). At that moment, veiled by darkness and in the stillness, the earth quaked and the rocks split opening them to the elements:

Then, behold, the veil of the temple was torn in two from top to bottom; and the earth quaked, and the rocks were split, and the graves were opened; and many bodies of the saints who had fallen asleep were raised; and coming out of the graves after His resurrection, they went into the holy city and appeared to many. (Matt. 27:51–53)

Jesus's last cry makes the earth tremble and Jerusalem vibrate. Then the Son of God expired His last breath and, "yielded up His spirit" (v. 50). Notice the cross itself stood safe and the only effect of the earthquake appears to be that of the rocks and graves opening, yet nothing else was disturbed. There were two effects of this unexpected quake; (i) *rocks rent*: not just cracks but great fissures i.e. chasms and splits in the rocks which laid the tombs open and their content discernible; (ii) *graves opened*: this was in the graveyard where Jesus was later buried in Joseph's tomb, which was close by. These sepulchres which had been excavated from the rocks were split open by *supernatural* energy. It was Jesus's voice that made the earth tremble and earth's crust shake. Not the earthquake or other natural forces, which tells us that it was altogether a *miraculous* act of God. As Nicholson puts it, 'it is brought about by the interference of God'.[3] So we can conclude that this event was not normal and not the result of natural forces but an independent act which by-passed the established natural order. As Nicholson writes again, 'The disturbance of a graveyard has a distinct place and importance of its own in the Calvary miracles. Indeed, in certain regards, it is the most remarkable of all we have yet considered.'[4]

THE SHOUT OF VICTORY

The open tombs were an earnest (foretaste) of things to come and even now they invite us to hope that the graves of all future saints will opened when the same Voice, that let forth 'a shout' of power then will do it again at the last day and the dead in Christ will rise never to die again:

For the Lord Himself will descend from heaven *with a shout*, with the voice of an archangel, and with the trumpet of God. And the dead in Christ will rise first. (1 Thess. 4:16)

The shaking of the tombs and the trembling ground brought fear to all who witnessed Jesus's death that day, 'when the centurion and those with Him, who were guarding Jesus, saw the earthquake and the things that had happened, they feared greatly, saying, "Truly this was the Son of God!"' (v. 54). This surprising and alarming event induced fear and is a harbinger and echo of a time yet to come. It too will engender fear. The Second Coming of our Lord will be ushered in by Kingly *shout*, now held in reserve, to precede Christ Jesus's decent a second time at the commencement of the Day of Judgement. These who are without faith and hope are prophesised to pray to the mountains and rocks:

Fall on us and hide us from the face of Him who sits on the throne and from the wrath of the Lamb! For the great day of His wrath has come, and who is able to stand? (Rev. 6:16–17)

4. When Jesus died resurrection was sealed

The final and fourth miracle of Calvary is in some ways the most remarkable of all and also the most mysterious. It follows on after the three hours of darkness; the tearing of the temple curtain and the earthquake which opened graves in Jerusalem's necropolis:

The graves were opened; and many bodies of the saints who had fallen asleep were raised; and coming out of the graves after His resurrection, they went into the holy city and appeared to many. (Matt. 24:52–53)

- It was not until *after* the resurrection of Jesus that the occupants of these tombs were raised and went into Jerusalem where they appeared to many. The Bible does not say whether these risen saints died again or went to heaven with the Lord Jesus. By His atoning death Jesus Christ destroyed the power of death and opened the gate of eternal life. By means of His own death we see and understand that that by itself did not complete the plan of redemption. Only by His bodily resurrection were death and the fear of death defeated, and by His once and for all victory over death the door of life eternal was set wide open. Resurrection from the dead by the man Christ Jesus is the seal of Salvation. When were bodies of the saints raised? It is important to note this: the narrative reads, 'and the graves were opened; and many bodies of the saints who had fallen asleep were raised; and coming out of the graves after His resurrection, they went into the holy city and appeared to many' (vv. 52–53), i.e. at the point or just afterwards, 'Jesus cried out again with a loud voice, and yielded up His spirit' (v. 50).

As to the question with what kind of body was given to the people that appeared out of their tombs? There are two main views.[5]

VIEW 1

The many saints who were raised were not corpses wrapped in grave clothes to die again, but witnesses to the promised hope of resurrection found in the prophecy of Daniel 12:2. They appeared to many and were 'made known' as real persons once deceased but now risen for the dead with bodies like unto Jesus Christ risen body (this view is held by commentators; William Hendriksen, Matthew Hendry and David Brown) and although Jesus was the firstfruits of those raised from the dead (1 Cor. 15:20) this does not make that invalid.[6] Only a real resurrection would proclaim Jesus as victor over death. Otherwise their resurrections 'would not be a foretoken of the glorious resurrection at Christ's return' for only a real resurrection would symbolise our future bodily resurrection.[7] Hendriksen adds, 'Is it reasonable to believe that these saints with glorious resurrection bodies remained in the darkness and corruption of the tombs from Friday afternoon until Sunday morning? The meaning is, in all probability, that theses saints were raised and left in their tombs at the moment of Christ's death.'[8] David Brown, on the other hand thinks the graves were opened as a preliminary event by the earthquake and the dead saints were raised on resurrection morning and he agrees that, 'this was a resurrection, "once for all to life everlasting"'.[9] These saints cause great wonder and astonishment but they did not die again having been raised 'who did partake of his first resurrection, a second death had no power'.[10]

VIEW 2

F W Grosheide suggests that these may have not been real resurrections at all.[11] However, others suggest that 'bodies of the saints' were raised as natural bodies and not with final resurrection glory. They were like Lazarus at his resurrection and as others revived, such as Jairus's daughter (Matt. 12) and the widow of Nain's son (Luke 7), who afterwards died a natural death to await the trumpet sound of resurrection. These people, it is suggested, could not have received their final resurrection bodies. This is more likely because they, as contemporaries of the people who saw them, where recognised and remembered. Mary Magdalene, Mary the mother of James and Joses, and the mother of Zebedee's sons were also witnesses to that event along with 'all His (Jesus) acquaintances'; who together recognised the bodies of the saints (Luke 23:49). However, this negative is less strong when we realise that the Saviour was recognised as Jesus of Nazareth who died and was crucified after He had appeared to the women and the disciples.

WHICH IS VIEW IS CORRECT?

There is much mystery here but let us acknowledge what is clear, all *except* Hendrickson and those above say the saints rose on Sunday morning but Hendriksen on Friday and only appeared later in Jerusalem. This latter suggestion would mean that the tombs lay open with the corpses exposed until after Jesus own resurrection on the Sunday. However, what is clear is that:

- Jesus destroyed the power of death and opened the gate of eternal life. Death entered because of sin and is the penalty for transgression; nevertheless Jesus died alone and exhausted sin's death-power satisfying God's justice and took the cure for sin and death on His own body on the tree.
- Jesus's promise of resurrection victory is illustrated by these miracles. His death has set wide open the door of eternal life and secured resurrection hope and blessedness for all who trust in Christ and His gospel.
- Jesus's loud *shout* (v. 46) was the moment of gospel victory over this fallen world.
- Only true saints alone will rise to eternal life, 'many bodies of the *saints* who had fallen asleep were raised' (v. 52).
- Jesus alone saves; we can add nothing to His work, 'He breaks the power of cancelled sin, *He* set the prisoners free' as Charles Wesley's hymn says.

The fact that rocks were rent seems to support the second view. They were rent as evidence of *force* however; their opening was also an evidence of *design*, which was, 'the budding of the coming glory'.[12] The opening up was not necessary for true resurrected bodies to gain freedom from death. Jesus Christ the firstfruits rose independently of the stone being rolled away. However, when Lazarus was raised Jesus said, 'Roll away the stone.' This was necessary as the revived bodies were locked in their burial chambers. Jesus own tomb was seen to be open for *effect*. It was an indication for the early witnesses to see with their own eyes that the person they expected to be where they had laid Him was missing and 'risen indeed'.

Conclusion

Around 2,000 years ago when Jesus Christ was crucified, miracles happened and dead persons became alive but only after the Saviour Himself had risen. Jesus is the firstfruits of those that 'sleep' so the mentioned unnamed saints who were given bodily resurrection were sharing in His victory over death and Satan (1 Cor. 15:51–53).

Remember that a 'better resurrection' is scheduled at the second coming (Heb. 11:35, 40). That resurrection event helps to add weight to the evangelical conclusion that we shall all be raised together—the whole body of believers from all ages, generations and continents. Thus in the fullness of time at His coming, and in a moment in the twinkling of an eye, at the last trumpet the dead in Christ will be raised (1 Thess. 4:16–17).

The earth's eternal state is called 'the new heaven and a new earth' where sin and death will be completely excluded. John's vision on Patmos sees the holy city, the New Jerusalem, coming down out of heaven, prepared as a bride adorned for her husband (Rev. 21:2).[13] The New Jerusalem that comes out of heaven is plainly distinct from the earthly Jerusalem, the former capital of Israel. This is the city Abraham looked for as the city that has foundations whose builder and maker is God (Heb. 11:10). This is the city that exists even now in heaven, for Paul calls it, 'the Jerusalem that is above' (Gal. 4:26).

Miracles

However we understand this passage of infallible Scripture, we are, after all is said, talking about miracles. A miracle, it can be said, is the 'visible suspension of the order of nature' and it is God intervening and acting immediately by an act of His will.[14] God can use the established order of nature to fulfil His will in a supernatural way. He *also* can intervene by suspending that order by an act of His will. Creation is open to His intervention. The world is God's creation. And He is greater than nature and is able to break into the present world-order because He is not an impersonal force but eternally divine. C S Lewis put it thus, 'If God creates a miraculous spermatozoon in the body of a virgin, it does not proceed to break any laws ... [Thus] a miracle is emphatically not an event without cause or without results. Its cause is the activity of God: its results follow natural laws."[15] Others have correctly said miracles are, 'extra ordinary [visible] acts of divine power'.[16]

NOTES

1 William R Nicholson, *The Six Miracles of Calvary* (Chicago: Moody Press, 1928), p. 16.

2 This was not the first time in history that darkness covered the earth in a supernatural way. Exodus 10:22 speaks of the ninth plague in Egypt lasting three days but not in Gotham.

3 Ibid. p. 51.

4 Ibid. p.64.

5 Help is received from: William Hendriksen, *The Gospel of Matthew* (Edinburgh: The Banner of Truth Trust, 1974), p. 975, n. 894; Matthew Henry's, *Commentary on the Whole Bible*, Vol. 5, (London: Pickering & Inglis, no date), p. 432; David Brown, *The Four Gospels* (London: The Banner of Truth Trust, 1969), p. 129.

6 Hendriksen, *The Gospel of Matthew*, p. 975, n. 894.

7 Ibid. Matthew Henry's, *Commentary on the Whole Bible*, Vol. 5, p. 432.

8 Ibid. Hendriksen, p. 976.

9 David Brown, *The Four Gospels*, p. 129.

10 Ibid. Henry's, p. 432.

11 Ibid. Hendriksen, p. 975, n. 894.

12 William R Nicholson, *The Six Miracles of Calvary* (Chicago: Moody Press, 1928), p. 65.

13 The Greek: *(Ierousalem kaine)* denotes a *new* Jerusalem i.e. what is *new in quality*. The New Jerusalem is better in quality. The old is full of sin and is temporary but the *new* is purified and eternal.

14 William R Nicholson, *The Six Miracles*, pp. 21–22 .

15 C S Lewis, *Miracles: A preliminary Study* (London: Geoffrey Bles, 1959), pp. 73–73.

16 E J Carnell, *An Introduction to Christian Apologetics* (Edward Carnell Library), p. 249.

Bibliography

Andersen, Francis I, *Job: An Introduction and Commentary* (Nottingham: Inter-Varsity Press, 1976)

Baxter, Richard, *The Saints' Everlasting Rest* (London: E Grant Richards, 1907)

Boettner, Loraine, *Immortality* (Philadelphia, PA: Presbyterian and Reformed Publishing, 1979)

Calvin, John, *Commentaries: Ezekiel*, Vol. XXI (Grand Rapids, MI: Baker Book House, 1979)

——, *Daniel* (Edinburgh: Banner of Truth, 1986)

Campbell, Iain D, *On the First Day of the Week* (Leominster: Day One Publications, 2005)

Chantry, Walter, *Call the Sabbath a Delight* (Edinburgh: Banner of Truth, 2000)

Chrispin, Gerard, *The Resurrection: The Unopened Gift* (Leominster: Day One Publications, 2013)

Edwards, Jonathan, 'The Perpetuity and Change of the Sabbath', *Works*, Vol. 2 (Edinburgh: Banner of Truth, 1974)

Gaffin, Richard B, *The Centrality of the Resurrection: A Study in Paul's Soteriology* (Baker Book House, 1978)

Gilfillan, James, *The Sabbath* (Edinburgh: A Elliot and J MacLaren, 1861)

Hendriksen, William, *Survey of the Bible* (Darlington: Evangelical Press, 1995)

Henry, Mathew, *Commentary on the Whole Bible*, Vol. 3 (London: Pickering and Inglis, no date–c. 1971)

Hodge, Charles A, *Commentary on the First Epistle to the Corinthians* (London: Banner of Truth, 1964)

Hoekema, A A, *Behold He Cometh* (Grand Rapids, MI: Reformed Free Publishing Association, 1974)

——, *The Bible and the Future* (Exeter: Paternoster Press, 1979)

——, *The Four Major Cults* (Grand Rapids, MI: Paternoster Press, 1969)

Humphreys, Colin J, *The Mystery of the Last Supper* (Cambridge: Cambridge University Press, 2011)

Josephus, Flavius, 'Antiquities of the Jews', *The Works of Flavius Josephus* (Edinburgh: Peter Brown and Thomas Nelson, 1836)

Kevan, Ernest F, *The Resurrection of Christ: Dr G Campbell Morgan Memorial Lecture, Booklet Number 13* (Glasgow: Pickering and Inglis, 1961)

Knecht, Glen, *The Day God Made* (Edinburgh: Banner of Truth, 1995)

Lee, Francis N, *The Covenantal Sabbath* (London: LDOS, 1969)

Lenski, R C, *I and II Corinthians* (Minneapolis, MI: Augsburg Publishing House, 1963)

——, *Acts of the Apostles* (Minneapolis, MI: Augsburg Publishing House, 1961)

Morison, Frank, *Who Moved the Stone?* (OM Publishing, 2001)

Murray, John, *Collected Writings*, Vol. 1 (Edinburgh: Banner of Truth, 1982)

Pipa, Joseph A, *The Lord's-Day* (Fern, Ross-shire: Christian Focus Publications, 2001)

Bibliography

Prime, Derek, *The Ascension: The Shout of a King* (Leominster: Day One Publications, 1999)

Ryle, J C, *Expository Thoughts on the Gospel of John*, Vol. 3 (London: James Clarke & Co., 1996)

——, *Expository Thoughts on the Gospels, St Luke*, Vol.2 (London: James Clarke & Co., 1969)

Sookhdeo, Patrick, *Is the Muslim Isa the Biblical Jesus?* (McLean, VA: Isaac Publishing, 2012)

Weber, Keith, *The Lord of the Sabbath* (Leominster: Day One Publications, 2007)

Wilson, Daniel, *The Lord's-Day* (London: LDOS, 1988)